IN UTOPIA

ALSO BY J. C. HALLMAN

The Chess Artist

The Devil Is a Gentleman

The Hospital for Bad Poets (fiction)

The Story About the Story (editor)

IN UTOPIA

*Six Kinds of Eden
and the Search for a
Better Paradise*

J. C. HALLMAN

ST. MARTIN'S PRESS ⚏ NEW YORK

www.stmartins.com

Image credits can be found on page 273

Design by Fritz Metsch

Library of Congress Cataloging-in-Publication Data

Hallman, J. C.
    In Utopia : six kinds of Eden and the search for a better paradise
    / J. C. Hallman—1st ed.
        p. cm.
    ISBN 978-0-312-37857-8
1. Utopias in literature.   2. Utopias—History.   I. Title.
    PN56.U8H35 2010
    809'.93372—dc22   2009047016

First Edition: August 2010

10   9   8   7   6   5   4   3   2   1

Acknowledgments

Far too many people to list here proved invaluable in the production of this book. A few deserve special recognition.

George Witte spotted the potential of the project, and Michael Homler lent it wisdom, a keen eye, and a firm pen.

Rob Spillman, Heidi Julavits, and Peter Manseau offered excellent advice on excerpts that appeared in *Tin House, The Believer,* and *Search,* respectively.

I'm quite lucky to have an agent, Devin McIntyre, willing to put out one fire for each fire I start. He has also taught me a thing or two about writing, which is as high a compliment as I know how to pay.

Last, this book would not have happened at all without Lynn Laufenberg.

I'm indebted to each of you, and to many more besides. If Utopia ever arrives, I'll invite you all to my home there.

IN UTOPIA

A JOKE

Only in us does this light still burn, and we are beginning a fantastic journey toward it, a journey toward the interpretation of our waking dream, toward the implementation of the central concept of utopia. To find it, to find the right thing, for which it is worthy to live, to be organized, and to have time: that is why we go, why we cut new, metaphysically constitutive paths, summon what is not, build into the blue, and build ourselves into the blue, and there seek the true, the real, where the merely factual disappears—incipit vita nova.

—ERNST BLOCH,
The Spirit of Utopia

I

Utopia is in a bad way.

2

Utopian thought can be broadly defined as any exuberant plan or philosophy intended to perfect life lived collectively.

As Ernst Bloch suggested, the historical drive toward utopia is best understood as a kind of light, or fire. Utopian thought sparked in antiquity with descriptions of fancifully perfect countries in Plato and Aristotle, smoldered like a coal mine fire through the Middle Ages with early monasticism and portraits of Eden and Heaven, burst into eponymous conflagration with Sir Thomas More's *Utopia* in 1516, caught and spread across Europe with religious fervor for 150 years, tacked for a century and turned secular, flared anew with the American Revolution and the French Revolution, burned like wildfire through the nineteenth century, and forged at last the ideologies that squared off in the twentieth century for what Thomas Mann called "a worldwide festival of death, this ugly rutting fever that enflames the rainy evening sky all round." Utopian thought bears its share of responsibility for that scorching of the face of the earth. As a word, it had already acquired a pejorative connotation, but after World War II "utopia" was no longer just a synonym for naïveté. It was dangerous. Now, decades further on, in a new century and a new millennium, earnest utopian thought and earnest utopians are a glowing ember at best, and utopia's legion failures seem to suggest that the best course of action would be to crush it—to snuff it for good.

By any rational measure, I should suggest this myself. But I won't.

3

This is a photo of my brother, Peter, and me in the backyard of our home in a master-planned southern California community in 1972. For six years we lived on a street called Utopia Road.

I'm there on the left, looking a bit too proud of those pants. The hopefulness of Utopia Road is apparent in the staked landscaping, but the dirt on the ground reveals the place isn't even finished yet. I like it that the bike's wheels sit right on the edge of the photograph. I'm perched on the rim of the picture's contained little world.

As a rule, utopias slip. They slip in the transition from conception to implementation; they slip as a result of financial expedience or frail psychology. Utopia Road had slipped from the ambitions of the likes of Frederick Law Olmsted and Ebenezer Howard's Garden City movement. By the time it filtered down to us the promise of a better life through better suburbs was hogwash. Considering for a moment only its internal effects, the vast shelter of Utopia Road, its informal biosphere, left its children safe but stunted, pure but uncertain. We were innocent, but in for a fall. Utopia Road housed us, but did not raise us.

There are a number of dichotomies in the image of my brother and me. The contrasts of our hair and our shirts, for example. I don't want to foist an agenda on a simple effort at documentation (the angle of the shot suggests the photographer was my sister, Amy, age ten), but various features of the picture's subjects do appear to offer commentary on their context. Peter's erect stance and his hands lodged firm in his pockets suggest the certitude and resolve of a homesteader, whereas my looser pose and my foot ready to crank down on the bike's pedal fairly screams out for abandoning a utopia already turned dystopian. The fashions of the image—the fifties fins on my Schwin, our sixties hair and seventies clothes—straddle a cultural revolution characterized by a rekindled, albeit narrowly focused, utopian spirit (i.e., free-love communes). Finally, my brother's annoyed squint and my goofy grin offer contrasting critiques: Peter intends to stick it through the hard times to make utopia work, while I'm ready to zip out of the frame even with training wheels and an untied shoe.

Like the picture, the history of utopian thought and literature refracts a broad range of dichotomies: rich versus poor, rural versus urban, past versus future, war versus peace, wilderness versus civilization, high-tech versus low-tech.* Even the name is half a duality. In the preface to *Utopia*, More explained that *utopia*, Greek for "no place," would become *eutopia*, or "good place," whenever some earnest visionary proved able to realize its dream.

There was no earnest visionary responsible for Utopia Road. It wasn't ever meant as a good place; it was a scheme to make a buck. The name Utopia Road was some real estate developer's idea of a joke.

4

The idea of a joke is central to the history of utopia—or at least to my version of it.

More borrowed from a broad range of classical and contemporary sources in the creation of *Utopia*, striking them together as flint stones to ignite the utopian blaze. But just how seriously

---

* Frank Manuel's definitive and indispensable *Utopian Thought in the Western World* offers a somewhat more academic list: "The body of utopia has been chopped into the soft and the hard, the static and the dynamic, the sensate and the spiritual, the aristocratic and the plebian, the figurative and the social, the utopia of escape and the utopia of realization, the collectivist and the individualist."

he meant the exercise to be taken has long been a matter of conjecture. The influence of *Utopia* is undeniable. No quixotic adventure, no bureaucratic catch-22, no charming Casanova, nor even any odyssey home is as universally recognized as the name of the perfect world we forever chase, the bittersweet flavor of hope. Among words that have leaped from fiction to reality, advanced from noun to adjective, it stands alone. But what did More mean by it? Theories characterize the age in which they are professed better than they characterize More or the book. Yet it's not going out on a limb to suggest that the history of the world since 1516 is a protracted history of not getting the joke of *Utopia*.

An inability to tell whether he was just kidding describes Thomas More's personal life as readily as it describes his book. Famous for his wit, More's friends were quick to note that a taciturn air made perceiving his humor no simple task. He apparently enjoyed this. More's arid nature is palpable today. Does the poker-faced expression of Hans Holbein's famous portrait of More disguise a nut flush or a lowly pair? Does More have you beat, or is he bluffing?

Holbein had been recommended to More by the famous humanist scholar Desiderius Erasmus. Erasmus described More's humor as prodigious. As a boy, Erasmus wrote, More was so delighted with puns he seemed "born for them alone." Erasmus served as More's confidant during the writing of *Utopia*; the two were lifetime friends. The inspiration for Erasmus's *In Praise of Folly* (1509)—a play on More's name, *morus* means "fool" in Latin*—arrived while Erasmus was on horseback on his way to visit his friend. The book, a joking treatise on the stoicism of the age, was written in seven days once he was installed in More's home.

Utopia borrows from *In Praise of Folly* as surely as it borrows from Plato. Like the entire genre of literature that would follow in its footsteps, *Utopia* is episodic and didactic, shifting freely between discourse and description. The book's structure is itself a dichotomy. Part one is treatise in the form of Platonic dialogue. Part two is travelogue in the spirit of the diaries of Amerigo Vespucci, published eight years before More set to work.

5

Utopia is set in the New World. A handsome island nation with fifty-four towns that suspiciously match the fifty-four counties of England, the country had made of itself a vibrant society despite an absence of natural resources and a pagan worldview. Utopians are happy, safe, fulfilled, and ready for the

---

* More himself composed Latin verses punning on his own name: "You are foolish if you entertain any long hope of remaining here on earth. Even a fool can advise you, More, on this score. Stop being foolish and contemplate staying in heaven; even a fool can advise you, More, on this score."

Christian message once it arrives in the form of traveler Raphael Hythloday, who spends five years in the country. A griz-
zled sea captain, Hythloday later returns to England where,
one day, he falls into conversation with fictionalized versions
of More and his group of friends. For a time they debate the
nature of the best possible commonwealth—private property
or no—and discuss whether good-intentioned souls should
willingly become counselors to their kings. More and his friends
insist there is no state better governed than England; Hythloday disagrees. They challenge him to offer one better.

After a recess for lunch, Hythloday describes the island of
Utopia—from the broad strokes of its geography to the details of
its governance. At the end, the fictional More is hardly convinced
that Hythloday has won the point. He dismisses a variety of Utopian laws and customs as "really absurd," yet concludes the book
with a statement that seems designed to enhance its ambiguity:

> Meantime, while I can hardly agree with ev-
> erything [Hythloday] said . . . I freely confess
> that in the Utopian commonwealth there are
> very many features that in our own society I
> would wish rather than expect to see.

6

The bulk of *Utopia* was written as a way to kill time during
stalled trade negotiations More was conducting in Bruges and
Antwerp. Part one—the discussion of service to one's king—
surely reflects the fact that during the writing of the book More
was offered an annuity to join the royal service permanently

under Henry VIII. It wasn't an easy decision. More was a successful lawyer; the job would be a pay cut. More important, service to anything was a sacrifice of autonomy, and how could he be sure that as a counselor to the king he would amount to anything more than a court jester?

Utopia amounts to a duel among jesters. The book is replete with Greek and Latin puns that would have stood out as though embossed on the page to its humanist-schooled intended audience. "Utopia" is the most obvious of these, but "Raphael Hythloday" runs a close second: The name, in degrees of free adaptation, translates as "nonsense speaker" and "bullshit artist." Hythloday's seagoing caricature was a hint that his character should be understood, as one commentator noted, as "the Jester's part in the comedy of *Utopia*." The fictional More—*morus*, the fool—was another. *Utopia* is a dichotomy of jokers.

Which must have made it frustrating for its author when readers began to ignore the obvious signposts and take *Utopia* literally. The deluge of imitators—the genre now counts hundreds of novels that borrow the book's template but ignore its irony—would not begin for a few years, but it became apparent almost at once that some had failed to get the joke. More publicly offered a gentle suggestion that certain readers might consider revisiting the text to more fully evaluate its myriad details. Privately, he lashed out at those who remained cold to the book's searing humor: "This fellow is so grim that he will not hear of a joke; that fellow is so insipid that he cannot endure wit."

This last was a real problem. For literature, More claimed, was by far the most effective way to achieve "a good mother wit." And wit was "the one thing without which all learning is half lame."

More's later history would make little difference in how the book came to be perceived. He spoke out against the communism that *Utopia* seems to endorse (as undersheriff of the city of London he was more Sheriff of Nottingham than Robin Hood, though he did have a reputation for fairness). He participated in Lutheran-burning even though Utopians practice religious tolerance. And he was eventually executed for refusing to sanction Henry VIII's divorce from Catherine of Aragon, even though divorce is permitted in his perfect world (H. G. Wells, an earnest utopian himself, later characterized this refusal as "reluctance to play the part of informal table jester to his king"). But More lost control of his creation long before he lost his head, and the very innovations that caused certain readers to mistake *Utopia* for a plan were precisely the things he had wanted to mock or indict. In his later years, he explicitly distanced himself from the book. After Thomas Müntzer quoted *Utopia* during the Peasant War to justify communal property More suggested that both *Utopia* and *In Praise of Folly* be burned.

Yet at the same time it must be noted that More seemed to enjoy the nighttime dreams he had during the book's production—dreams of himself as King Utopus. His regal self was taller, he wrote to Erasmus, and he was quite satisfied manning the helm of the Utopian ship of state. He held his head high. He marched down the street in a diadem of wheat and with a scepter of corn, and was accompanied by his nobility in the task of meeting ambassadors and princes of other nations—all poor creatures by comparison.

So was *Utopia* criticism of the England it resembled? Was More applauding an imaginary nation that employs shrewd statecraft and common sense to defend itself with the least harm to others? Or was he criticizing a misread of Machiavelli just as *The Prince* was being published, and calling for a government that would compensate for human fallibility with divine inspiration?

No one really knows.

Excepting perhaps the Bible, there is no work that is simultaneously so influential and yet so difficult to pin down as to its precise purpose, or even its nature. This work does not aspire to solve the riddle of *Utopia*. I am not a utopologist (and there are such things), nor can I say that I am utopian in any specific sense of the term. But I was weaned on utopia, and after it became for me more than a word on a street sign, utopian novels began to crowd my bookshelves. To write a book that emulates *Utopia*'s toggle between analysis and what scholars call its "speaking pictures"—in other words, to borrow the episodic strategy of the genre—is, for me, on one level, an attempt to produce a definition of myself. On another it's an investigation of wit. More's wit, it has been suggested, was intended to "correct, chastise, wound." But to what end? Wit is a straight line without a finisher, without a punch line. You, reader, supply your own. For five hundred years the world has stood dumb before the wit of *Utopia*. In the picture of my brother and me on Utopia Road, it seems as though I've gotten the joke, as though I've got a punch line in mind. My boy's good humor is already attuned to More's irony:

Which makes me, perhaps, an unlikely vehicle for the message of this book: the utopian flame should not be snuffed—it should be stoked anew. The history of utopian thought sheds a light on civilization that both illuminates and scalds: Civilization triggers utopia, embraces it—then indicts it. The stigma now attached to utopia not only fails to get the joke, it blames hopefulness for hope's failures. Utopia critiques crisis. It acts. To crush the utopian spirit would be to extinguish the campfire just as its warmth is needed most.

Winter closes in: Is being saved worth the risk of being singed?

A WILDERNESS

It is impossible to understand history without utopia, for neither historical consciousness nor action can be meaningful unless utopia is envisaged at both the beginning and end of history.

—PAUL TILLICH,
"Critique and Justification of Utopia."

For no man can write anything who does not think that what he writes is for the time the history of the world.

—RALPH WALDO EMERSON,
"Nature," *Essays: Second Series*

8

I was up in the Gila National Forest of southwestern New Mexico, straddling the Continental Divide above ten thousand feet—locals like to say you can walk to Canada from here, as though you can't from anywhere else—and I was hiking into the Aldo Leopold Wilderness, the first officially designated wilderness in the United States. Leopold, the father of wildlife management and a founding member of the Wilderness Society, once had been labeled utopian for arguing that outdoor America should be rebuilt with the same political tools that destroyed it. More pressing for me, he'd also said that wilderness wasn't really wilderness unless it could "absorb a two weeks' pack trip." I was only an hour into his reserve, but still I was starting to get a little freaked out. This wasn't entirely my fault. For the last several weeks I'd been communicating with a band of renegade scientists, perhaps utopians themselves, and the point had been made to me a number of times that the thing missing from wilderness these days was big animals and fear. So I was zigzagging between views of the entire eastern half of the continent on one side and the entire western half of the continent on the other, huffing and puffing in the thin air and gazing out across the land's crumpled carpet of pine, and I was thinking about animals that were large enough to eat me. I was about fifty miles from a crappy little town called Truth or Consequences, and it felt like it. So far, the only actual animals I'd seen were lizards whose frantic push-ups revealed that in no way did they regard me as an apex predator. Everything was peaceful, serene, sacred, etc., but still I started to get a feeling that I get only when treading in deep dark water. I started to feel like prey.

A primal wilderness might actually be a good place to begin a study of utopian thought, as, arguably, utopian thought itself begins with Christian conceptions of untrammeled country: Eden, Promised Lands, Heaven on Earth. The Bible, in fact, may be the source of the word "wilderness," though strictly speaking it splits the difference on it. It's the place we should conquer (Genesis 1:28), but it's also where Jesus finds wisdom (Matthew 4:1) and Elijah and Moses find guidance (I Kings 19:4, Exodus 19:3). It's what Adam and Eve are cast into (Genesis 3:22)—making Eden more Utopia Road than *Utopia*—but God lives there, too (Exodus 3:18, 7:16).

Some version of this contradiction explains why, though I could comprehend that being afraid of wilderness was a good thing, my imagination was screaming at me to get out of there. Specifically, I had begun to consider the mountain lion, which, because suburban sprawl has been encroaching on its territory for decades, has been known to stalk and kill people. As I approached a peak a variety of unfortunate scenarios involving lions and myself played out in my mind. I decided to scribble a few notes and head back to the car.

I sat on a boulder, my back toward a sharp incline. The work went fine for a while. There was no burning bush to dictate any primitive constitution, nor was it for fear of God that I had stopped, but still I rejoiced: The mountaintop offered a visceral sense of the earliest of utopias. I had scraped up against a remnant of some still-golden age.

Then I felt a low grumble behind me. I froze, my pen mid-sentence. The feeling, the sound, slipped up my neck. I began to turn, and the mountain flat out exploded. New Mexico does have defunct volcanoes, so this wasn't such a crazy thought, though really I was expecting a vise of jaws on the back of my neck. But when I got all the way around there was only the harsh light of the sun, and a sonic blast of a roar, and then, just a couple hundred feet over my head, the outline of a military jet flashing over the treetops. It was no lion—just some jar-head asshole buzzing the watershed in the oldest wilderness in America.

I had come to be frightened of animals, but wound up scared of what was essentially myself.

9

A few years after Amy snapped the photo of Peter and me, our family moved to another house in the same town. For convenience I'll continue to refer to this town as Utopia Road, though that was not its name.

The external effects of Utopia Road were apparent by then. Early on, wilderness had surrounded the small civilization we had chinked out from the California chaparral. On the bus ride to school I could look into the hills and spot coyotes surveying their encroached-upon territory. Their morning routine was to watch our morning routine with their trickster's scaled-back dignity. The basic sales pitch of modern suburbia claims that this juxtaposition of civilization and nature makes for a kind of unity, a "marriage of town and country." But by the eighties rampant growth had caused a flop, and our sterile neighborhoods had laid siege to the last scattered pockets of scrubland. Utopia became dystopia. The coyotes vanished.

Wherever one goes, it seems, that flub in civil calculus tends to coincide with the emergence of local wildlife rehab programs, amateur hospitals fueled by good will. Animals that fail to beat a hasty retreat to whatever angular flakes of wilderness remain either wind up as roadkill or turn up injured in backyards. Before long just about everyone finds themselves standing over a bleeding and helpless raccoon, wondering whether there's anyone to call who knows what to do.

In Utopia Road, there was someone who knew what to do. Marge and Tom Knothe had started out modestly, helping a friend care for wayward songbirds, but soon they graduated to injured kestrels and owls they kept in their screened-in porch. Before long they had a complex of two-by-four-and-chicken-wire enclosures in their backyard to care for opossums, pelicans, and hawks that people brought them. The Knothes were both schoolteachers; they had no real training in caring for animals that often came in injured well beyond the hope that they could ever be returned to the wild. Their one-level ranch had more than an acre stretching out behind it—a wilderness in the California real estate market—and in the heyday of what became known as the Wildlife Rescue Center they cared for a total of sixty-eight different species. They took on teenage volunteers and a motto: To Be Wild and Free.

Peter volunteered at the Center for two years before I was old enough to follow in his footsteps. Marge and Tom were weary souls by then. Tom had lost an eye to illness and tilted his head when he looked at you, like those pelicans, and Marge had a weak heart after a decade of shouldering the entire community's guilt. At fourteen I volunteered on Thursdays and weekends, cleaning opossum cages, chopping up chicken parts for the raccoons, and pureeing baby mice for invalid hawks, blending them to a solution we called "Pinkie-Colada." Even before I arrived the Center had flowed over with permanent residents, and the place was part farm, part asylum, a purgatory where injured animals, sinless as cherubs, waited out their end time. Marge and Tom were pleading publicly for help by then, and the Center was on the brink of disappearing like the land it hoped to save. I was the last volunteer at the Wildlife Rescue Center.

10

I started thinking about Marge and Tom again a couple of years ago when I read a scientific paper proposing something called "Pleistocene Rewilding." It was a crazy idea. North America during the late Pleistocene period was home to a menagerie of large animals—megafauna—that included ground sloths as tall as giraffes, diprotodons like one-ton wombats, tortoises the size of Volkswagen Beetles, and an array of lions, horses, elephants, and bears, all of which suddenly went extinct about ten or twelve millennia ago for reasons no one is certain about. Recent biological studies had proved that megafauna, predators in particular, were good for ecosystems, and the Pleistocene Rewilders—the paper had twelve coauthors—wanted to bring the lost animals back. They claimed man had a hand in the Pleistocene extinctions and that the continent had been left ecologically bereft—sterile, safe—as a result. Pleistocene Rewilding would rebuild what had been unwrought.

The paper caused a minor frenzy, first in the media (the authors landing on morning talk shows and finding themselves the target of clever headlines like "Lions and Cheetahs and Elephants, Oh My!" and "Beasts of Both Worlds"), then among academics who hated it ("obnoxious" and "nuts," two critics later told me). My problem was that I liked the idea. I liked it a lot. And I liked it precisely because it struck me as utopian: an impossibly positive action that stood in stark contrast to the dastardly suburban sales pitch. As a first step, the Pleistocene Rewilders had proposed "ecological history parks," experimental ranges populated with megafauna, which tourists would flock to, they claimed, for the same reason people flocked to the San Diego Zoo's Wild Animal Park. The Wild Animal Park was just five miles away from Marge and Tom's Wildlife Rescue Center.

And the impulse was the same, I thought. The instinct to fix what you've broken, whether by reducing greenhouse emissions or rewilding nature, was no different from the instinct to help a writhing raccoon or to turn your backyard into a labyrinth of pens. I began to investigate Pleistocene Rewilding and came to understand the beef some had with it. It didn't "re-" anything. Pleistocene Rewilding would create a world that had never existed, which was ill-advised. If the plan came to pass, the fear was, then the fate of the Wildlife Rescue Center might repeat, and the whole continent could wind up as a sad zoo imploding of good intentions.

All utopias run the risk of dystopia.

I didn't care. Hadn't I grown up in just such a failed vision? What was the alternative? What I hoped to discover was that a utopia could battle back against dystopian scourge.

II

As soon as I started digging into Pleistocene Rewilding— talking both to its supporters and detractors—I found the suburbs of San Diego and even Marge and Tom's songbirds down there among its roots.

When Thoreau, in "Walking," claimed that America was well suited to human habitation because it lacked "African beasts, as the Romans called them," he appears not to have known that the Americas once seethed with such creatures. It's ironic, then, that the arc of conservation begins with Thoreau; it then bends through John Muir and Aldo Leopold, a trajectory that measures a decline in quality of prose style, an increase in ecological understanding, and a tailing away from transcendentalism pretty much in line with modernity's drift from religion to science. If Thoreau was conservation's Adam, then Leopold was its Abraham. Leopold's "land ethic," which sought to change via fiat man's relationship with nature, was the single guiding belief behind the recently emerged science of conservation biology. For specific laws, conservation biology needed a Moses, and it found one in Michael Soulé, an academic notable for having once left academia completely to spend five years in a Zen Buddhist temple in Los Angeles.

Soulé was one of the coauthors of the Pleistocene Rewilding paper.

Soulé grew up not far from Utopia Road.

Like my brother and me, he had made a playground of the southern California wilderness, wandering from chaparral mesas to tidal pool systems, and later to isolated canyons between suburban developments. Conservation biology itself, he told me, when I called him in Colorado, had been kicked off at a conference in San Diego in 1979. As a student at Stanford, Soulé studied lizard evolution on California islands. Islands figured heavily in conservation biology, as it drew on island biogeography, a field pioneered in the sixties to explain species extinction patterns. At that point, biologists had begun to reject a long-standing belief that nature was all about stasis and balance. Island biogeography charted a measure of predictability within the new complexity. Nature as stasis was replaced with nature as predictable cycle of crash and reclamation, extinction and immigration.

Conservation biology, Soulé said, didn't really hit its stride until he emerged from the Zen temple. In a nutshell, it was a crisis discipline, like cancer research, that could offer scientific rationale for conservation action in the face of uncertainty. In 1985, Soulé published four axioms that became the science's guiding commandments:

1. Diversity of Organisms is Good
2. Ecological Complexity is Good
3. Evolution is Good
4. Biotic Diversity has Intrinsic Value

From there he returned to San Diego's isolated canyons. He began a study of precipitous declines in the populations of the same songbirds that Marge and Tom Knothe were keeping in shoeboxes across town. The entire scientific community agreed that the world was experiencing a man-driven crisis of species extinctions, and you could witness it here. Civilization was strangling wilderness. But could you prove it scientifically? It had been suggested that factors that made extinctions predictable on islands—size of landmass, distance from shore, etc.—might also apply to "habitat islands," isolated woods or nature reserves. Soulé used the songbirds to demonstrate that the mainland was predictable, too.

The culprit in the canyons, it turned out, was coyotes. Not too many of them—too few. Coyotes preyed on raccoons and opossums, which in turn preyed on songbirds, and when you removed the coyotes, raccoon and opossum populations soared and the songbirds crashed.

That was one example. A host of biologists were then in the process of confirming that large predators and other megafauna performed a "keystone" function, offering beneficial effects that cascaded deep through ecosystems. If you wiped out a keystone species, biodiversity decreased and evolution stopped. A solution loomed: Put them back.

"At first glance," warned an early text, "a vision of North America with regained wildness and biodiversity seems unrealistic, even utopian."

But it worked. The crown jewel of "restoration ecology" was the reintroduction of wolves to Yellowstone Park in 1995. Controlling moose and elk that had been overgrazing for decades, the wolves benefited themselves, willows, beavers, ravens, grizzlies, pronghorn antelopes, and songbirds.

13

But then came Pleistocene Rewilding, with its plan to bring back animals that had been gone for thirteen thousand years. This was a leap of faith. You couldn't bring back saber-toothed tigers or ground sloths, but you could introduce "surrogates," African lions or rhinoceroses, that did the same ecological "job." For some, this alone made the plan hopelessly utopian. Even Soulé once wrote that "a cynic might describe rewilding as an atavistic obsession with Eden."

"One of the skills ecologists learn," he told me, "is to look at an ecosystem and see what's missing, what's not there. And what's missing is large species. I always felt the absence of large species was the ghost lingering in our ecosystem. That accelerated when I started looking at birds in canyons. That's what lit the fuse of my concern."

Soulé lit my fuse. I decided to go to the Southwest, where the original meeting of the Pleistocene Rewilders had taken place, and where many of them lived. I arranged to visit a few of the principals. Before I left I searched online for Marge and Tom Knothe. A quarter century had passed—nothing. I turned to a piece of satellite mapping software that would have struck an earlier age as an advance of utopian dimension. From my desk I launched a preflight across the trip I would take, whooshing over the continent like an astral journey. The Knothes' speck of land would be worth millions if they had not chopped it up for more homes. I zoomed in on Utopia Road, soaring over old haunts at hawk height. The neighborhoods had changed; swimming pools winked aqua up at the orbiters. I steered through data and memories.

I found it, intact—they were still there.

14

In the case of nature in general, and animals in particular, the standard criticism that utopia slouches toward tyranny appears entirely justified.

A belief that fewer animals make for better living is apparent even in accounts of prehistoric golden ages. A Sumerian epic set in the fourth millennium B.C. is nostalgic for a time predating the appearance of "noxious" creatures.

> *In those days there was no snake, there was no*
> *scorpion, there was no hyena,*
> *There was no lion, there was no wild dog, no*
> *wolf,*
> *There was no fear, no terror,*
> *Man had no rival.*

The shift from a golden age to utopia amounts to a transition from longing for a paradise lost to trying to make a new one. Man's adversarial relationship with nature remained for thousands of years—until the twentieth century, really—and once the un-got joke of *Utopia* ignited, the battery of manufactured perfection and a dim view of the natural world made bad news for animals.

Utopian novels that followed in the wake of More in some cases prescribed and justified annihilation.

> ... the equally important advantage of having rid the country of almost all the animals that were dangerous to man or harmful to agriculture.

> It seems a law of nature that animals not useful to man gradually recede from the domains he occupies, or even become extinct.

And in others claimed that no lasting ill effects would result from the ongoing spread of civilization.

> The beauty and romance of nature are exposed to no danger whatever of being destroyed by the leveling instruments of future engineers.

Utopias suffer from understanding lag. Historically, utopias have failed because they do not fully account for the world's variety or complexity. Not surprisingly, then, a tendency to deny one's own utopianism is characteristic of utopians, and even today earnest utopians are not keen on being branded with the word.

15

Dave Foreman, founder of the ecoterrorist outfit Earth First! and another of the coauthors of Pleistocene Rewilding, was at best a reluctant utopian.

My trip began about as far from wilderness as you could

get, in the sprawl on the outskirts of Albuquerque, on a horrific strip of gas stations, convenience marts, and one cheap motel where I took a room. Foreman picked me up and drove us a mile into his suburban neighborhood, entirely average but for the automatic gate that stretched across his driveway. Inside he showed me his library and a kind of drafting room where he kept an exhaustive archive of maps detailing nature reserves in North America. Age and his back going out on him had slowed Foreman down from the wild old days. In moments of pause, he still tended to sink into a signature macho pose, but with his hair and beard gone gray, one had to say that he had embraced a kind of late Hemingwayness that accounted for his fascination with big animals, the look, and even the cat he had blamed for the typos in *Confessions of an Eco-Warrior.*

In his living room we uncorked some New Mexico wine. "Really, there are two kinds of rewilding," Foreman began, and just that fast he distanced himself from the more utopian vision of Pleistocene Rewilding.

Yet it was Foreman's own history that betrayed the idea's utopian lineage. He hurried through the oft told self-made myth of his life for me.

He was descended from folks of Daniel Boone–like pluck, and as a boy he had witnessed a fatal shark attack that was the creation story of his preoccupation with big critters. He had once attended officers' candidate school (sixty-one days total, half in the brig—authority issues, it sounded like) and campaigned for Goldwater, but he swung left as the traumas of the sixties unfolded. He took a formative *Easy Rider*–style road trip, and then wandered into destiny, stepping into the office of a New Mexico conservation organization. He landed in Leopold's Wilderness Society and found himself working as a lobbyist, elbow to elbow with senators and presidents.

Foreman remembered that the Wilderness Act of 1964 had netted activists a fraction of the protected space they requested, and he got screwed himself in the seventies during an effort to section off the few roadless areas left in North America. The Reagan revolution was the final straw. Foreman and a few friends formed Earth First!, which advocated the monkeywrenching of Edward Abbey's novel *The Monkey Wrench Gang*. Foreman penned *Ecodefense*, a how-to guide for tree-spiking, damaging heavy machinery, and "miscellaneous deviltry." Loosely orchestrating a movement of ecosaboteurs made Foreman famous, and pretty quickly attracted the attention of the FBI. He woke one morning to three agents with .357 Magnums standing around his bed.

But it wasn't the FBI that had gotten him second-guessing things, he said. By then he had already begun to suspect that Earth First! tactics had exhausted themselves. The purpose of the movement had been to make less radical conservation efforts—the Sierra Club, for example—look ordinary. That had been accomplished. If you vaulted too far down the path from pranks to terrorism, someone was going to get hurt— and they had. As well, Earth First! had become a culture— tribal and pagany—that Foreman wasn't comfortable with. At an event in 1986, he recalled, he and a friend found themselves sitting on a hill above a crowd of half-naked kids beating on drums.

"I'm not at home here," Foreman told his companion.

A short time later *The New York Times* characterized small

Earth First! towns among the redwoods as "isolationist utopias of neo-hippies."

16

Utopia offers a scathing critique of fencing-in wilderness—it
raises prices and helps spread disease among animals—but
the criticism is Hythloday's, so who could say whether it was
genuinely meant? Otherwise, the Utopians have no truck with
wilderness: Hunting is considered abhorrent and left to slave-
butchers, and they have perfected a kind of utilitarian land
management, uprooting whole forests and replanting them to
make logging easy.

A new kind of utopia less ambiguous on the wilderness
front emerged with the twentieth century's growing conscien-
tiousness toward nature. "Ecotopias" challenged the mess left
behind by earlier utopias. Baker Brownell's *The Human Community* (1950) echoes Leopold's land ethic; poet Gary Snyder's
Turtle Island (1969) advocates a "world tribal council" and the
return of bison to the Great Plains; and Ernest Callenbach's
Ecotopia (1975) describes a latter-day secessionist movement that
makes a perfect ecological society of the northwest United States.
The sequel, *Ecotopia Emerging* (1981), depicts the reintroduction
of grizzly bears to the Sierras.

Over wine, Foreman admitted that ecotopian philosopher
Paul Shepard was central to the initial conception of Earth
First! In *The Tender Carnivore and the Sacred Game* (1973) and
Coming Home to the Pleistocene (1998), Shepard offered a pro-
posal even more radical than civil war.

The evils of civilization all lay at the feet of agriculture, Shepard claimed. Agriculture shifted our relationship with nature from symbiosis to dominance and created class divisions among people by implying private property. Better was the "Great Hunt" that occupied most of human history, from two hundred thousand to twelve thousand years ago. Citing the !Kung San of Africa, Shepard claimed that primitive peoples suffered through less work and anxiety and enjoyed more sleep and leisure than "advanced" societies.

"Our home is the earth," he wrote, "our time the Pleistocene Ice Ages."

Earth First! aped a slogan of Bring Back the Pleistocene.

Which is precisely what Shepard went on to propose. It started out sounding like More applied globally: 8 billion people would move to 160,000 cities of 50,000 inhabitants each spread out like a ribbon along coasts all around the world. The centers of each continent would return to the wild. Children would be initiated into adulthood with arduous excursions into that wilderness, and eventually all hunting would be conducted by groups of men using only hand weapons—danger would trigger a primal spirit. A "Pleistocene Paradigm" called for abandoning all domestic plants and animals and using only handmade tools.

Shepard later admitted that his vision was somewhat tongue-in-cheek—sort of a joke. Foreman's problem with Earth First! was perhaps that his followers didn't get it—they took it all literally. Foreman dodged the word "utopia" every time I brought it up. This annoyed me. He had difficulties with Shepard, he admitted. Foreman himself had once claimed the real utopians were those who believed it was possible to provide for everyone at current population levels.

But not all were so hooked on utopia in the pejorative. Paul Sears, a botanist who had once been Shepard's teacher at Yale, argued the opposite.

> It would be a grave injustice to dismiss utopian thought as mere fantasy, visionary and impractical. To consider it restricted to literary forms that bear its label is to underestimate its wide prevalence at many levels and in all cultures. However expressed, it is essentially a critique of the defects and limitations of society and an expression of hope for something better.

17

The ecowarrior had begun to grow a bit weary of his story, but I pressed on.

What he meant by two kinds of rewilding, he said, was that there was Pleistocene Rewilding and a less bold kind of rewilding based in land management. Truth be told, he preferred the latter.

This was the direction his career took after he left Earth First! In the early nineties, he teamed up with Soulé and conservation biology. By then conservation biology had set as its primary task the amelioration of the country's inefficient splatter pattern of protected space, its vast archipelago of habitat islands.

Foreman came along just in time to help with the Wild-lands Project, a movement that set as its goal the creation of "corridors," pathways for wildlife between existing reserves. Individual reserves could be linked with measurable benefits to evolution and biodiversity. There was a larger scale as well. Foreman wrote another book, *Rewilding North America*, and descended into his archive of maps to draw up four visionary "megalinkages" that would suture the continent's ecological wounds. The huge arrows swept across the land like invasion plans.

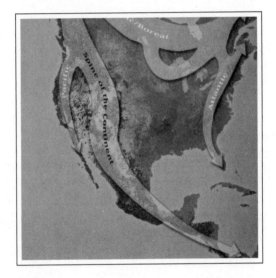

The megalinkages, I thought, critiqued the present and offered hope. But was it utopia?

For Foreman the more radical vision of Pleistocene Rewilding was like Earth First! It was a crazy plan that would make this other crazy plan look not so crazy.

It wasn't a joke, but he didn't really mean it earnestly, either.

I didn't challenge him on it. He was tired. He dropped me back at my motel.

18

He perked up again in the morning when we hit the road, heading northeast out of Albuquerque and swooping through hills rimmed with rocks and ponderosa pine. He was taking me to an "equid ranch" to visit a captive population of Przewalski's horse, which had gone extinct in the wild and which the Pleistocene Rewilders had suggested might make a good surrogate for lost American horses.

Horses demonstrated that Pleistocene Rewilding could actually work.

Several equid species had been lost in the Pleistocene, but ten thousand years later domestic horses were accidentally introduced to North America by the Spanish. Pockets of rewilded horses thrive today. Burros, too, introduced to the Grand Canyon by miners, had helped spread native seeds until bureaucracy caught up with them. In 1963, the Leopold committee—chaired by a son of Aldo—ruled burros nonnative because they had not grazed there within the previous five hundred years. Thousands were shot.

"Welcome to the Great Plains," Foreman said, when I woke from a nap. He was a little giddy now, anxious to see the Przewalskis, and as we got close, gliding past Wagon Mound, a little town at six thousand feet, he became wistful about the last time he had visited the wild horses, on a trip with a few of his co-authors. "Seeing them there on the ranch, on the high steppes, with the Rocky Mountains as a backdrop—they just looked so *right* there."

The equid ranch was surrounded by twenty-eight miles of electric fence. Its eight thousand acres made it far smaller than the million acres Foreman told me you'd need for a proper Pleistocene Rewilding experimental range. It was owned by an eccentric millionaire who had made his fortune, I'd been told, traveling the world in search of oil and gas. He had a thing for horses, Foreman said. The ranch had hundreds of endangered asses and zebras and sixty or so Przewalskis.

The ranch manager was a man named Hammer who was scruffy and fat and annoyed that we were an hour late. He asked me not to write about him. I agreed. Then he put up a ruse of not showing us around because we were late. I asked to speak to the millionaire. Hammer relented—he was kidding, he said—and he gave us a cursory look at the offices, the vet center, the hangar for the millionaire's plane. Then we headed off for a driving tour of the ranch, weaving through hypnotic patterns of curious zebras. We coasted into a labyrinth of juniper, idling past haystack-sized shrubs and their shadows. Hammer drifted to a stop in front of a few bushes.

"How many zebras you see back there?"

"One."

He smiled and held up five fingers. I looked back into the brush and my heart leaped a little when I began to spot eyes blinking out of the shadow-flage. I hated Hammer.

It took us a while to find the Przewalskis. They were a success story. Named for a Polish explorer, they had last been spotted in the wild in Mongolia in 1968. They could not be broken for labor. The animals alive today were all descendents of about a dozen individuals. The captive population had climbed steadily through the first third of the twentieth century, only to crash during World War II, when a number of animals died in the firebombing of Göring's hunting ranch. After the war the population climbed again, and successful reintroduction programs were begun in Mongolia and China.

We found two small bands of Przewalskis grazing out away from the zebras and asses. They were quiet and smallish and shy; mothers steered new foals away from our Rover. The Przewalskis were uniformly almond, with short black manes and a stripe running down their backs. Behaviorally, they were similar to domestic horses, but if it was possible to sense preening in domestic horses, some awareness that we found them beautiful, then the Przewalskis didn't really care. They were a James Dean of a horse—cropped hair, vaguely cool, accidentally beautiful, and entirely untamable.

And sad in that way, too, caged as in *Rebel*, beaten as in *Giant*. I didn't see the grandeur Foreman saw, and I didn't see the Rocky Mountains in the distance. I saw fences. Foreman sat behind me in the Rover, gawking and snapping pictures. The equid ranch, I thought, was another broken hospital, like Marge and Tom's mad asylum. The horses required supplemental feeding; it wasn't enough land.

Foreman and I traded moods on the ride back to Albuquerque. He was excited now. All that was left of his biography was the sunset he imagined for himself.

"I just want to go down into the Gila Wilderness Reserve, take an overdose, and let the ravens pick at me," he said, smiling.

"Don't you want to be cremated? Reenter the cycle of things?"

"Nope! Go the whole way with it."

Not quite Hemingway.

19

The problem with Pleistocene Rewilding boiled down to a dichotomy: species introductions versus species *re*introductions.

Reintroductions of wolves to Yellowstone or birds to island groups had produced positive, repeatable results. But introductions—placing an animal in a system where it had never been before—were themselves a major cause of extinctions: ecodystopia. New Zealand and Hawaii were the classic cases. New Zealand had a total of three mammals before people arrived, all bats, and had since been invaded by 34 land mammals, 33 bird species, 1,600 plants, and 1,500 insects. Local biodiversity crashed irrevocably. The attempt to set things right by introducing additional species, such as predators to control pests, generally made for a comedy of errors. Hawaii introduced mongooses to control rats—hoping to protect songbirds—only to discover that mongooses are diurnal and rats nocturnal.

The problem with the introduction/reintroduction dichotomy was that no one could say for sure where you should draw the line between the two. The Grand Canyon burros had done just fine contributing to local biodiversity until they hit the "pre-Columbian curtain." Everything on this side of the curtain was "recent," the argument went, and animals that had been lost recently could be reintroduced. But what ecological logic was there for Columbus? It was an arbitrary designation—

narcissistic and possibly racist. Why not move the curtain back to the Pleistocene?

20

The real utopian of Pleistocene Rewilding—the earnest utopian—was not Dave Foreman or Michael Soulé; it was a retired zoologist named Paul Martin.

In 1961, Martin had been one of a group of young scholars to accompany Yale ecologist Ed Deevey on a trip to Poland to attend a conference. Deevey was familiar with Martin's romantic plan to bring back lost species. Didn't think much of it. But that changed on a field trip when Deevey glimpsed a herd of bison roaming free in a Polish forest. The next afternoon, Deevey later wrote, "in a heady postwar atmosphere, a good deal more reminiscent of Hemingway than of Conrad," Martin joined Deevey for lemonade at a Warsaw café. For Deevey, that conversation was the birth of the "overkill hypothesis," Martin's claim that the Pleistocene megafauna had gone extinct due to hunters who arrived in North America at just about the same time the animals vanished. Could man be culpable for the Pleistocene extinctions? Did it mean we should tear down the pre-Columbian curtain? Perhaps, Deevey thought. But in 1961 it was still premature to consider "repopulating Arizona, say, with horses, camels, elephants, antelopes, tapirs, and peccaries—for we have one witless menagerie in New Zealand and scarcely need another."

Nearly half a century later Martin still smarted from his teacher's words. His own hopes had fixated on the return of the elephant. In a 1999 essay called "Bring Back the Elephants!"

he claimed that the return of "the Proboscidea [was] by no means as witless as it might seem at first." He cited data from Africa that demonstrated elephants controlled brush, regulating fire, and dug for water, which helped many other species. He called his plan "resurrection ecology."

It took another five years, a new name, and a little help from Ted Turner to get the idea moving at all.

In 2004, after Martin and a couple others brainstormed the proposal for the Pleistocene Rewilding paper, they needed space for a meeting. Laughed out of academic venues, they turned to Turner, whose much praised endangered species fund worked with wolves, grizzly bears, prairie dogs, ferrets, and trout.

The Pleistocene Rewilders used one of Turner's large ranches in New Mexico as a gathering place. The twelve coauthors included predator experts and paleoecologists, an intentional blend of sympathizers and cynics. The talks started testy but ended with agreement. The most skeptical among them were appeased with language in the paper specifying a contained experiment as a starting point. This was left out of the media deluge that followed. One of the morning shows included an animated clip depicting elephants marauding through Manhattan. Ted Turner called his ranch manager as soon as he found out about the plan, furious at the suggestion that he would be bringing African animals to New Mexico.

The tortoises didn't bother him so much. After the media hype fizzled, it turned out that the first animal that would burst from the Pleistocene Rewilding gates was a turtle. The coauthors had suggested that a captive population of endangered Mexican Bolson tortoises could be bred and introduced to those places in North America where fossils showed they had lived eight thousand years before. In other words, the Bolsons, then wild only on a small and shrinking parcel of land in Mexico, could be saved by a Pleistocene curtain. The captive population was currently housed at the Appleton-Whittell Research Ranch, a reserve a few hours south. Turner was interested, and a plan was hatched to bring the tortoises to his property.

21

I made for Turner's ranch. South of Albuquerque, the land opened up. When a train passed in the distance I could see all of it at once, a fat worm needling forward on the desert floor. Mirage spilled sky into the funnel mouth of the road ahead of me. Two hours south, I drove eight miles of twisty road inside the ranch, only to be told I'd passed through just the southern tip of it. The ranch was 255,000 acres—seventeen times the size of Manhattan. Not far away Turner owned another ranch three times larger than that.

The manager was an elegant gent named Dobrott. Dobrott drove me out onto the range where the tortoises would be kept once they were moved up from the Research Ranch. The land was unremarkable, but the range would amount to a minirewilding experiment, including bison, pronghorn, prairie dogs, burrowing owls, and the Bolsons. The size was still small—another eight thousand acres. Fencing would separate the animals.

Dobrott had participated in the Pleistocene Rewilding meeting, but eventually he asked that his name be removed from the list of coauthors. He didn't want to explain this. One of the more curious arguments I'd heard from the critics of

Pleistocene Rewilding was the claim that it amounted to ecological colonialism. Africa couldn't provide for its wildlife, it
seemed to suggest, and the United States, even as it threatened
to sully its most pristine regions to sate its oil thirst, would
care for the world's animals. It was hubris. I came to understand this only as Dobrott mused on the Bolsons while steering us back to ranch headquarters.

"This is really a Mexican project. The Mexicans just don't
know it yet."

He meant the pre-Columbian curtain was fine where it was.

Dobrott had to get back to work. The Turner ranch was then
in the process of culling its bison herd to purify its genetic
makeup. Dobrott seemed content with this: The ranch was a
kind of gene bank. Keep the species, keep them pure. Someone
else will make the withdrawal.

"That's my life's one little contribution to 'rewilding.'"

22

From Turner's ranch I swung west and chased Foreman's suicide plan into the Gila and the Aldo Leopold Wilderness. I got
buzzed instead of awed, was more annoyed than inspired, and
came back down from the mountain with nothing at all etched
in stone—only my half-scrawled notes. I drove farther west
into the Gila, and before long I received another man-made
jolt: the Santa Rita open-pit copper mine. It appeared around a
bend, several thousand acres of artificial moonscape, the dirt
tiered up around the mine mouth so that the site was flanked
by stories-high pyramids of gray soil. It sat there, biblical in the
wilderness, tipping the scale for me. Pleistocene Rewilding

might have been hubris, but I didn't care. I wanted someone to do it. I didn't want Foreman's trick, some strategy to cajole people into whatever was right, and I didn't want a joke either. Neither Marge and Tom's modest sanctuary, nor the equid ranch, nor Turner's projects were on a proper scale. I wanted a North Dakota polka-dotted with bison, I wanted elephants doing the job of ground sloths in Arizona. When the science of biology emerged, when they started counting and realized just how many species there were in the world, biblical scholars hustled to recalculate the length of a cubit. What we needed now was a project as audacious as Noah's. We needed a bigger boat. The Pleistocene Rewilders had been criticized as unscientific, but what they hoped to achieve, on a scale of dozens to hundreds of years—the same scale Shepard imagined for his Pleistocene utopia—was the intangible balance that lurked beneath nature's chaos and was too complex to fully measure or describe. How *could* it be a science?

Only a utopia could reply to a crisis of dystopian proportion. If anything, the Pleistocene Rewilders hadn't asked for enough. It was precisely because I knew dystopia that I knew a utopia was called for in reply.

23

"The Paul Shepard argument is a big one," Donlan said.

The lead author of the Pleistocene Rewilding paper was not any of the highly respected names that filled out its list of co-authors. It was Josh Donlan, an up-and-coming biologist who had not yet finished his Ph.D. Though Donlan lived in a yurt off the grid, a tent nestled up against one mountain and looking across a plain at a whole range of them—not so differently from Shepard's future primitives—he wasn't talking about the philosopher's Pleistocene Paradigm. He was citing Shepard's claim that you could witness our reverence for animals, for large carnivores, in our tendency to name sports teams after them. However, judging from the drawings in Paul Martin's original book on the Pleistocene extinctions, I had to conclude that the extinct creatures looked less like sports team animals and more like sports team mascots.

From the Gila I had driven south into the Sky Islands, a series of forty mountain ranges at the meeting point of four major ecosystems, one of the most biologically diverse places in the world. Donlan's yurt sat on the foothills of the Chiricahuas, looking across the San Simon Valley. Geronimo had been born here. The yurt was one part survivalist camp, one part sheikh tent—propane oven and refrigerator, log-burning stove, and a comfy living room where we sat when I arrived.

Donlan was thirty-three and fairly dashing for a scientist, a contrast to his co-authors, whom he called "ecological silverbacks." He was a nomad, living at the yurt four months out of the year and traveling the rest of the time to a variety of projects, most notably one just then being completed on the Galápagos Islands. In 1997, Donlan and a few friends formed Island

Conservation, an NGO that worked on eradicating introduced pest species from island chains. The Galápagos project targeted seventy-nine thousand invasive goats that had been driving to near extinction birds and tree-sized sunflowers that went back to Darwin's time.

Eradication had helped make rewilding seem possible—get rid of the pests, reintroduce displaced species. But an animal doing well isn't so easy to get rid of, and eradication had become its own discipline. Contending with their witless menagerie, the Kiwis were pioneers, and Donlan had brought them in to help with the goats. The first 90 percent were easy, he said. You just hunt them. Finding the last 10 percent was the trick. The solution was a "Judas goat": Capture a female, spay her, give her hormones to make her horny, put a radio collar on her, and release her—goats are social.

Which makes the point that biologists these days aren't exactly what you'd call animal lovers. "We're not purists, we're pragmatists," Soulé had told me, and Donlan's own pragmatism emerged when our talk turned to the critics of Pleistocene Rewilding.

"We're not going to have runaway Bolson tortoise populations. We're not going to have runaway lion populations. If we do—we killed them once, we can do it again."

From the yurt we could see twenty or thirty miles across 270 degrees of horizon. Out on the plain I counted four dust devils, hundreds of feet high, toiling their separate troubles. Donlan described the Turner ranch meeting, the hush that fell across the room when certain attendees spoke their minds. The group was full of "rock stars," Donlan said. He gestured out a tent flap to the Peloncillos across the valley when I asked who might be able to implement a Pleistocene Rewilding experiment. A few leagues away lived a group of conservation-minded ranchers who had the land and weren't inclined to sell out to developers. Another possibility was Native American tribes that didn't want to give in to casinos. And then there were the Texas game ranchers who had already imported seventy-seven thousand exotic animals—for hunting. They were all long shots.

I tagged along as Donlan checked mouse traps for a study he was conducting on animal movement between ecosystems. He pinched the captured mice carefully, measured their feet, and tagged their ears if he hadn't caught them before. They bounced away. Back at the yurt he cooked us bison burgers from Turner's ranch.

"Will Paul Martin be disappointed if he never sees an elephant in the wild?"

"After the meeting at the ranch, Paul told me he was going to die happy." Donlan thought a moment about the realities of conservation. "Most people at the ranch—they won't see an elephant in the wild. *We* might."

24

The Research Ranch lay between Donlan's yurt and Paul Martin's home in Tucson, not far off the Buffalo Soldier Trail on the way to Fort Huachuca.

There's a New Mexico joke. Why is the land around Trinity site, ground zero of the world's first atomic detonation, healthier than 95 percent of the state? Cows are worse than nuclear bombs.

When Coronado rode through this part of the country in 1540, bringing cows with him, he reported that local grasses stood as high as his horse. The eight thousand acres of the Research Ranch had been permitted to go wild for three decades, and grasses were exactly what I found when I pulled past the fence on its border. The land shifted at once from stoney, shit-brown dirt spotted with half-dead mesquite and vapid Holsteins to fields of wheat-colored stalks as high as the car windows. The land felt bounteous, and the motion of the grass in the wind gave it the character of flesh.

I met a woman named Chaun Copus for a tour of the Bolson tortoise pens. Copus was past sixty and had worked with the tortoises for twenty years. She was sorry they were leaving. Copus had a live-wire reputation. She wore a desert camo hat, a T-shirt with the sleeves rolled up over her shoulders, a walking cast and a plastic slipper, diamond earrings, red lipstick, sunglasses, and a gun.

It wasn't the best time of day to observe the tortoises, but we found a few out sunning. The most remarkable of the bunch was a basketball-sized matron as old as Copus herself. The little beast regarded us with Triassic suspicion. Copus tried a tortoise call.

"Hey, Gertie, Gertie, Gertie!"

The tiny dinosaur shimmied down into her burrow.

I spent the afternoon walking the reserve. I found an immense dead sycamore, leafless, bark flaked away, exposed wood like muscles on a naked giant with a thousand arms. It was June, over a hundred degrees. Like the Buddha, I tried another tree and concluded shade was the reason the Buddha started sitting under trees in the first place. It was quiet for a time, and I heard two airplanes, far from each other, the sound of their engines twining together as in a dogfight. My hand touched a bit of garbage, blown or carried in: a page from a cell phone manual, in Spanish.

25

"It's a question of which side of the fence is natural," Paul Martin said, when I told him I'd just come from the Research Ranch. "Different politics spin off different interpretations of that."

Martin was a big, frail man. Polio had hobbled him in 1950, but I'd seen photos of him spelunking despite the useless legs. We were in his home office. Its walls of books were higher than the room was long. Martin sat cozy in a wheelchair. His memory of the Pleistocene was better than that of his own past. His eyes smiled at me all on their own.

What he meant about the Research Ranch was that neither side was actually natural. The problem with cows was not that they were cows. The problem was that they were fenced. They did not move freely across a range. Martin was thinking, probably, of the fire-regulating service of his elephants. Unchecked grasses become a hazard if nothing ever eats them down. Crash and reclamation. Even the Research Ranch was a hospital.

High on a shelf I spotted a parcel marked "Feces Bovine."

"Paul, did someone send you cow shit in the mail?"

"I hope so."

I asked him to explain his theory, his plan, but a lifetime of academic squabbles couldn't be reduced to a well-crafted speech. He talked for a while about drill cores, mammoth kill sites, pollen in the fossil record, and how Coronado hadn't seen any bison when he brought his cows into Arizona.

I reminded him that his old teacher Ed Deevey had once claimed their meeting in Warsaw was the beginning of it all.

"Yeah, yeah. I was waving my arms and talking about over-kill as the only sane way to interpret what happened."

"So overkill first occurs to you in Poland."

"We could say that."

I asked how the idea for the Turner ranch meeting came about.

"Probably some phone calls. Who's the guy I know, retired now? Boy, I hate this short-term memory. He worked for Turner."

"Joe Truett?"

"Joe Truett. Joe Truett was as influential as anybody when I started talking about this. He knew people at the Turner foundation. They wouldn't have to endorse what we were going to do, they just had to approve the list of people, and the subject matter, more or less."

I reminded him that Turner hadn't been too happy about Pleistocene Rewilding.

"Well, I didn't worry about that. That was Donlan's department. Hey, I don't need to worry about the future. Josh is leading the charge."

"How did the meeting go?" I asked.

"Well, the Bocks could see that a guy like Foreman was going to be open to this idea. And of course there was Berger, and Josh, and Harry. And who else?"

"Soulé, Burney, Estes, Felisa Smith—"

"Estes I don't think was there. Wanted to be. Anyway, he's in the group. He works with the people who work with whales.

And sea otters. And everything in between. That's provocative. The sea cow, and what it's doing, and the whole idea that ecosystems are interacting in dynamic ways. Because sea otters are affected by predation in big marine mammals. Under certain conditions, they take a big hit. That kind of dynamic gives us a sense of what it would be like to have a management of elephants. You have to know your animals. Might take some Indians who are good at managing Indian elephants to get it started. It might not be so easy to work our way into African elephants. I don't know. But I do know that this continent without elephants is not wild America."

"There's a big jump from talking about Pleistocene Rewilding to doing it."

"Yeah, huge jump. Really, it's a matter of patriotism. What is right for our country, and what is, given the political realities of the time, our proper management approach."

"Do you consider Pleistocene Rewilding utopian?"

Martin eyed me for a moment. "Well, it's idealistic. It has no predecessors. I don't know that Paul Shepard would like it. But it may be utopian. We're talking about resurrecting elephants out of the Old World and putting them back into a continent where they once were, when there may be good reasons they're not there anymore. As I see it, we're just seeing if there are any fish down there. Here's the bait, here are the lures, and it's a murky-looking pond. Are there any fish down there?"

"Who are the fish?"

"People like Turner. People of means. They have a terrible problem with the amount of resources they have, and wealth, and power, and influence. People who are wealthy and have influence often love the out-of-doors. Creative ways to move into the out-of-doors might appeal to someone because they know that operating in this realm requires what they have. This is one of the most neglected areas in the natural sciences. Look at the money thrown at extraterrestrial exploration—a woman comes on the television, an undergraduate, she's mapping landings on Mars. This is where the focus is going. So we're trying to capture some of that, looking backward in a totally new way, to challenge people to think about doing things on Earth that are doable. To create a richer environment than we have now. To argue that way."

26

From Tucson, I headed for Utopia Road. I did not return to my old neighborhood. Instead, I drove to the Wildlife Rescue Center.

Marge and Tom were home—they had never left. Tom still cocked his head to look at you. Marge had let her hair grow long and loose, and she no longer played Fagin to our town's crew of privileged lost boys. They remembered my brother but not me. I took them to lunch, and they gave me a tour of what they'd been doing with their acre in the twenty-five years since the Wildlife Rescue Center collapsed. They had rewilded it. They had yanked out all the invasive species and reintroduced boulders with Tom's pickup. They planted local species—elderberry, white sage, deer grass. "The wilder, the better," Marge said. She had managed the plot into regions: desert, chaparral, riparian, oak woodland. They had a pond, and a stream to keep it irrigated. Oregon grape, sumac, coyote bush. Someone who remembered the old days had brought them an opossum recently—they released it under their palm trees. Monkey flower, chemise. "We never go anywhere," Marge said. "There are so many people. If I want to go somewhere, I go into my backyard." Quail bush, artemesia. They had built utopia, and the animals had come—they had seen coyotes on the property. Mule fat, chiparosa. Not long ago a mountain lion had found its way here. A panicked neighbor made a call. Desert lavender, juncus. It was hunted down and shot.

A COMMUNITY

It has justly been said that in a positive sense every planning intellect is utopian.... In the face of all this, which makes "society" a contradiction in terms, the "utopian" socialists have aspired more and more to a restructuring of society; not, as the Marxist critics think, in any romantic attempt to revive the stages of development that are over and done with, but rather in alliance with the decentralist counter-tendencies which can be perceived underlying all economic and social evolution, and in alliance with something that is slowly evolving in the human soul: the most intimate of all resistances—resistance to mass or collective loneliness.

—MARTIN BUBER,

Paths in Utopia

27

Any sympathetic overview of utopian thought must acknowledge itself as utopian in conception.

I tried to join utopia.

28

The modern "intentional community" evolved through waves of utopian fascination in the 1790s, 1840s, and 1890s. A range of men carved for themselves niches in history by inspiring communal efforts that rose up heroically only to collapse over base human emotions: greed or jealousy. The stigma now attached to utopia is largely the result of the failure of the commune model—in macro as communism, in micro as remote communal living units—to establish lasting purchase.

B. F. Skinner ignored all that.

In 1945, between the fall of Germany and the bombing of Hiroshima, Skinner paused to take stock of society. He had just finished a productive year on a Guggenheim fellowship building the science of behavioral psychology. Any pleasure he might have taken at the prospect of peace or his own professional advancement was tempered by disappointment at witnessing his wife and her friends struggle through the toil of domesticity and the humiliation of listing "housewife" as previous employment on job applications.

"Was there not something to be done about problems of that sort?" Skinner wondered. "Was there not by any chance something a science of behavior could do?"

There was. Skinner had once considered becoming a writer (as a young man he had sent a batch of short stories to Robert Frost, who praised them), and by his own account he produced a utopian novel with just such a goal, *Walden Two*, as a way to kill a few spare months before taking the chair of a university department in Indiana.

Accordingly, the protagonist of *Walden Two* is a Professor Burris who, with a few colleagues in tow, makes a skeptical visit to a community founded by a former student, Frazier. (Skinner's first name was Burrhus, and the characters' initials—B and F—are said to represent his ambivalence toward communes.) Earlier communal movements, the utopian Frazier tells his visitors, failed because their populations always wanted *more*. The trick was to make them want less. His impassioned speeches on how human values can be molded through "behavioral engineering," a murkily described process in which positive reinforcement "forces" right thinking, seduce some of his visitors and enrage others.

"You're a dictator after all," Professor Burris tells him.

"No more than God."

Walden Two was a peculiar title choice. Thoreau had once rejected an invitation to join a gathering of transcendentalists— "As for these communities, I think I had rather keep bachelor's hall in hell than go to board in heaven"—and the whole point of behavioral engineering seemed to be to eliminate civil disobedience.

The book received little attention until another spark of

utopianism caught in the 1960s. Skinner was tenured at Harvard by then, and he tracked rapidly growing counterculture interest in *Walden Two* with meticulous charts monitoring sales. In 1966, without Skinner's participation, a conference was convened in Ann Arbor with the expressed goal of establishing a real Walden Two community.

29

A young woman named Kat Kinkade attended.

Kinkade's imagination had been fired by utopian literature since she was a teenager, but it wasn't until she'd lived a mainstream life (marriage, job, child, divorce) that she considered creating an alternative herself. At thirty-four, she was assigned *Walden Two* in a philosophy extension course. She fell in love with Frazier. He was the man she'd been dreaming about her whole life. By the time the Michigan conference was convened, Kinkade had already tried forming her own urban commune.

The conference failed—the Ph.D. organizers imagined themselves "psychologist-kings," Kinkade said later—but it did bring together a core group of people who set out to establish a Walden Two community in the Virginia woods in 1967. They called the experiment Twin Oaks. It was one of a handful of communities that attempted to use Skinner's utopian novel as a how-to manual.

"Because we have *Walden Two*," Kinkade wrote, five years into the project, "we do not need a leader or teacher."

Historically, five years was already better than most communes. But Skinner was not the only utopian pitching community in the sixties, and Twin Oaks attracted as many Skinnerians as it did hippies looking for free love. The subtext of control in *Walden Two* generated friction. Skinner's influence was eventually abandoned. Kinkade gave up on Twin Oaks. She left the community to found another in Missouri and to work alongside Skinner in Boston for a few years. Twin Oaks refused to die. Kinkade returned in 1982, staying for a decade and a half. By then Twin Oaks was America's longest-lived secular social experiment, and Skinner was a memory.

From there, Kinkade's story took an ironic turn: She left the community again, and like Thoreau chose to live in a house by herself not far from Twin Oaks. She was still there.

30

My visitor group gathered in the Twin Oaks guesthouse living room to establish the "social norms" we would observe for the duration of the three-week visitor period required of applicants. There were ten of us: three college students from a left-leaning school a couple of hours away; two young women with dreadlocks; one ex-con massage therapist; one fairy godmother–like divorcée; one ex-clown; and two writers, including me, though I didn't reveal that to any of them.

The meeting had been scheduled for us three days into the visitor period. So far, our response to being thrown into small living quarters together was a naïve interpretation of anarchist philosophy: We ignored the sign that read "Please Leave Shoes at Door," and, like children, left clothes lying all about. The meeting was our introduction to intentional society, and would amount to a group hashing-out of policies for simple things like cleaning protocols, as well as stickier items like public nudity and frequency of toilet flushing. Twin Oaks had not become a nudist colony—though it was common enough to spot bare-breasted women working the garden fields—but as an egalitarian community it had to accommodate whatever one might prefer. An area outside the main dining facility, for example, was reserved for those who wished to dine both al-fresco and au naturel, but naked lunches were frowned upon by some, and we had noticed signs warning against the spread of pinworm.

The other writer in the group, a tall lanky scholar of politi-cal science, called us to a loose order. Earlier, I'd heard the scholar announce that he was planning to teach a class on uto-pias someday. "There are just so many ways to go with it," he said. In truth, I felt a little threatened by the scholar. Like me, he was sampling a social experiment so as to conduct an ex-periment of his own. That was why he was anxious to get us organized. But it turned out he wasn't content to just set us in motion and watch. When it started to sound like we would adopt Twin Oaks's liberal policy of open bathroom doors, he be-came agitated.

"Here's how it's going to be with me. When I'm in there doing my business, that door will be locked. When I'm in the shower, it will be open—come get your toothbrush, whatever. But it's locked when I'm doing my business."

This policy was ratified with silence.

The divorcée said she had a problem with "excessive" nu-dity. She was an older woman from the Bay Area, and she had been reading about Twin Oaks for forty years. A few months back her overbearing physicist husband had served her with papers, and now she was branching out again. The divorcée was full of stories of wilder times from her youth, casual ménages à trois and brushes with latter-day Beats, but marriage had left her a docile woman, and she was probably uncomfortable with the matron's bulk that had resulted. She presented her concerns as hygienic, however, and I sensed that some of the younger crowd, the ex-clown and one of the college students, an innocent girl child of two bird colonels, were disappointed. Another of the students—a former acrobat whose perfect breasts were the subtext of this whole portion of the conversation—seemed relieved.

"Leave your pinworms at the door," I offered, to explain the divorcée's position.

"Exactly."

We compromised on limited nudity.

The meeting was "creditable" work. Twin Oaks still operated on the "labor credit system" Skinner had suggested in *Walden Two*. Already we had begun putting in labor shifts, learning the basics of the community's two main industries, hammock making and tofu production. In each of our three weeks we would log a certain number of hours to "make quota." This was true for members, too, who received an allowance of about two dollars per day in exchange for a workweek of forty-two hours, though "work" included things like providing child care, being sick, hanging your laundry, and attending meetings.

We hurried through the business of shoe storage, window management, and general cleaning but got stuck again on toilet flushing. The room fell silent until a young philosophy student sat up.

"There's an adage," he said, pausing for gravitas. "When it's yellow, leave it mellow; when it's brown, flush it down."

"Well," the divorcée said, "when it's yellow, close the lid."

The final order of business was how much labor we would award ourselves for the meeting. One of the dreadlocked girls, a recent college grad who had turned down a Fulbright to try to join Twin Oaks, had spent time here as a guest a few months before and knew her way around more than most of us. She suggested that we chat for a few more minutes and give ourselves an even .5 hours.

The scholar stepped in, looking at his watch. "I'm not breaking the rules here. You all can take .5 if you want. I'll take .4."

That night a few of us sat around chatting, beginning to form the bonds of our small living group, or "SLG," as it was called in the community. The would-be Fulbright told a few stories that revealed the community's pervasive sexual vibe, and soon a few of the women were offering massages to one another. The scholar gave us his initial assessment: Twin Oaks was not a republic; rather, we were all living under a voluntary labor dictatorship.

"That's my working hypothesis. It's only been three days, but I don't think it will change."

I had my own theory.

31

Which required a little history.

The utopian novels that followed More eventually inspired utopian plans that were in no way intended as jokes. James Harrington's *The Commonwealth of Oceana* (1656), Thomas Spence's *Spensonia* (1803). Scholars recognize John Locke's constitution for the Carolinas as utopian in spirit, and the Declaration of

Independence and the U.S. Constitution are indebted to the utopian Levellers* of the seventeenth century and Harrington, respectively. Rights and practices now accepted as self-evident—freedom of speech; power-sharing government—appear as provocative suggestions in documents regarded as utopian when they were produced. Long before Skinner, there was frustration that talk of social reform tended to stop at that triggered action. Utopian thought became utopian experimentation. Book became blueprint. Central to the genealogy of Twin Oaks were three men whose societal systems were most prominently tested in the United States.

Born in 1772 to a French cloth merchant, Charles Fourier claimed to have taken an oath against commerce at five and to have had sexual intercourse at seven. (The latter led his biog-

raphers to conclude that he had had no amorous relations at all.) Fourier made his living as a traveling salesman but believed that he had divined God's true will—attraction. He proclaimed a kind of laissez-faire of the senses. Once humanity entered the "associative" phase of its existence (thirty-six phases total), he said, our most instinctive desires would prove also to be in the best economic interest of the community. In Fourier's perfect world, all the varied temperaments of mankind (810 temperaments total) would be brought

---

* "We the free people of *England* . . ." reads the preamble to the Levellers' founding document.

together in "phalansteries," great communal buildings like grand hotels. Here, God's true plan would be revealed through aggressive indulgence in sexual and gustatory appetites. Fourier remained at home until noon every day awaiting the generous capitalist who would fund his vision. None ever arrived.

Robert Owen—by contrast—was gentry attempting to share the wealth. Owen worked his way into the English cotton industry and married up, assuming control of his father-in-law's mill in New Lanark, Scotland. Just a year older than Fourier, Owen's philosophy began with the radical propositions that people were not fated by heredity or class and that man's character was shaped by society. In 1817, he announced an effort to renew New Lanark through education and a belief that individual happiness was linked to community happiness. His innovations were mild steps forward—children remained  in school until they were ten years old, instead of just six or seven—but New Lanark was counted a success. Owen's egalitarian streak advanced as the years passed. He later argued that the institution of marriage contributed to the stagnation of the species. His vision of a perfect community came to fixate on a population of two thousand living in a large castlelike structure.

Owen thought his system scientific. Marx and Engels agreed, and were particularly drawn to his de-emphasis of religion.

In 1824, Owen was approached by a sales agent representing
the Rappite religious community of Harmony, Indiana. George
Rapp was taking his Rappites back to Pennsylvania. The whole
town was for sale. Why not buy it, the agent argued, and test
your system in America? Owen agreed, believing that if the
transfer from Rappites to Owenites proceeded gradually, he
could replicate the success of New Lanark. "New Harmony"
would become the largest—eventually growing to nine hundred members—of about a dozen communities in the United
States to attempt implementations of Owen's system.

It didn't go as planned. When Owen arrived in Indiana the
Rappites were already gone. New Harmony was repopulated
with whoever responded to a cattle-call appeal for subjects in
a social experiment. For a year and a half Owen complained
about dishonesty and rampant drinking, and the community
split itself into subcommunities. Owen sold what land he could
to whoever was on it and returned to England. None of the
Owen communities lasted longer than three years.

Fourier communities did somewhat better—no thanks to
Fourier. Jealous of the attention Owen received, Fourier dis-
owned what meager attempts arose during his lifetime to
bring his vision to pass. His most significant contribution
to realizing his theories was a series of five-francs-per-hour
lessons he offered to newspaper columnist Albert Brisbane,
who went on to author a book introducing the system to America. Brisbane's Fourierism got a year's free press in *The New
York Tribune*.

At the same time, a group of prominent intellectuals—

spinning off unitarianism and transcendentalism—were embarking on a communal project at Brook Farm, Massachusetts. Margaret Fuller participated and Nathaniel Hawthorne visited for a time (the experience documented unflatteringly in *The Blithedale Romance*), and Emerson, who flirted seriously with joining, rejected membership when it was offered because he felt the communal enterprise demoted the importance of the individual. Thoreau's reasons were similar, though he had been less tempted at the prospect.

Brisbane's Fourierism caused a national stir, and a convention was held in Albany to attract adherents. The Brook Farmers converted in 1843, and the site quickly became the center of American Fourierism, a movement that included several dozen "phalanxes" ranging from New Jersey to Wisconsin. The Brook Farmers began work on their phalanstery: They planned a hundred private rooms, a dining hall for four hundred, two saloons, and a lecture hall. Though Fourier had claimed that his new domestic order would make fires a "matter of very inconsiderable consequence," a defective chimney released a stray spark not long into construction, and the entire phalanstery burned to the ground.

Brook Farm folded, and most of the phalanxes—for a variety of reasons—followed suit within a few years.

33

The best account of both the Owen and the Fourier experiments came from a man named A. J. Macdonald, who traveled to sixty-nine communities over twelve years, sat down with his notes, wrote a preface, and died.

His papers wound up in the hands of John Humphrey Noyes, founder of Oneida Community in upstate New York. Oneida picked up where Owen and Fourier left off, and eventually became the most successful social experiment of the nineteenth century.

Noyes concluded that Macdonald's book would have put socialism in a bad light. Noyes's own *History of American Socialisms* promised to make "better use of his materials" and went on to suggest that Oneida had "harmonize[d] Owenism and Fourierism" around their one common denominator: the extension of family beyond "the little man-and-wife circle."

Noyes had attended Yale Divinity School and married rich like Owen. He founded Oneida in 1848. Oneida counted itself "Perfectionist" and "Bible Communist." Citing Matthew 23:30,

which claimed marriage was not an institution of the kingdom of Heaven, Noyes claimed that sex for love was more important than sex for propagation. He coined the term "free love." All of Oneida was one "complex marriage," with everyone married to everyone else. There was a lot of sex—but few orgasms. Men practiced "male continence," climaxing only when attempting to conceive. The result was a permanent atmosphere of sex and the opportunity to practice "stirpiculture"—Noyes's word for eugenics. For years Noyes acted as "first father" to young women entering the complex marriage.

On a practical front, Noyes argued that if a community

hoped to survive it must position itself near a business center. Oneida did exactly that, and made its living from constructing steel traps, processing lumber, preserving fruits, making chain and silk thread, and handcrafting travel bags. Oneida lasted three decades before the community's second generation rebelled against complex marriage and Noyes both. Noyes left in 1877. Two years later the community was transformed into a joint-stock company, a child of the stirpiculture practice herding them into the mainstream. Oneida Ltd. eventually became well-known for the production of flatware. It declared bankruptcy in 2006.

34

Oneida failed as a commune just as utopian thought sparked again. Several dozen new communities came and went in the twenty years leading up to the turn of the century (Charles Gide noted renewed interest in Fourier in 1901), and scores of utopian novels either presaged or surfed the wake of what quickly became the most influential utopia after More, Edward Bellamy's *Looking Backward* (1888).

Both B. F. Skinner and Kat Kinkade cited Bellamy as primary source material.

Looking Backward begins with a man falling into a mesmerized sleep in a working chamber underneath his house in Boston. He is accidentally entombed when the house is destroyed by fire, and is discovered 113 years later, miraculously unaged and curious to "look back" on a century of progress. He is shown an America where credit cards have replaced money and an "industrial army" (the idea lifted from Fourier) has replaced the service class. All production is run by the government, and there is no war, no taxes, no crime, and no law schools. The book was a campaign for socialism that avoided the already stigmatized word.

In other words, *Looking Backward* signaled an advance. Now utopias could both present a speaking picture that criticized the present as well as offer an unironic blueprint for the future. *Looking Backward* was a runaway bestseller and inspired more than two hundred "Bellamy clubs" dedicated to installing its ideas. John Dewey, Eugene Debs, and Thorstein Veblen each acknowledged Bellamy a debt. A 1930s survey of prominent thinkers counted the book among the most important works of the previous fifty years, some listing it behind only *Das Kapital* in influence.

35

Which didn't mean it was any good. Bellamy was an undistinguished writer before *Looking Backward*, and followed up his success with an undistinguished sequel.

He shouldn't be blamed for this.

From a literary perspective, utopian novels are uniformly bad. It's not hard to see why. In a world without war, crime, or law schools, how does one generate dramatic tension? After More, the solution was the "utopian romance." The genre's guided tour of paradise is afforded tepid narrative drive by the addition of a quaint story of budding love. Utopian novels are romantic not just because utopia is unrealistic but because the only drama available to a story of a perfect world is sexual tension.

Which perhaps explains why Bellamy seemed a bit backward when it came to describing advancement for women—a common enough topic in early utopian plans. Bellamy too fooled with a love interest to keep his story moving: His hero falls under the spell of one Edith Leete, a descendant of (and dead ringer for) the love he left behind in 1887. He is thus keen to investigate the psychology of women of the future. "We have given them a world of their own," he is told. But all it really means is fewer household chores. True, stores have given way to vast distribution centers, but Edith is still an "indefatigable shopper." She spends most of the book arranging flowers.

By contrast, even Fourier had acknowledged that "the extension of privileges to women is the general principle of all social progress."

36

I had my own love interest.

My "significant adjacent cohabitator," as she preferred to be called, dropped me off at Twin Oaks three days before the social norms meeting. The cohabitator was brilliant and beautiful, not to mention a self-described communist, but it's fair to say she was somewhat concerned about whatever sexual tension I might discover at Twin Oaks. She regarded my experiment warily. She suspected I might not come home. From the visitor parking lot she peeked in at the community, feigned nonplussedness. She left me with an ironic peck on the cheek so as not to "cramp my style."

I was the first of the visitors to arrive. I checked in at the office on the main courtyard, a rough square of buildings shaped by the community's original farmhouse and the first few residences that had gone up as the population began to grow in the seventies. Hammock chairs hung around the square as though it were all a front porch, and like a symbol of utopia hammocks stretched between trees all over the farm.

I was escorted to the guesthouse by a member named Ted. Ted had grown up as a Mennonite, but it hadn't really stuck, and later I saw him conducting one of the public tours that the community offered on occasional Saturdays wearing a dress. He wasn't cross-dressing. Clothing had no particular association with gender at Twin Oaks, and men wore skirts about as often as they wore nothing at all. Ted would be relinquishing his membership soon, he told me. There had been a schism. The community had recently decided to invest several hundred thousand dollars in its tofu business, and Ted's plan for the construction of a new building had been passed over in favor of a more conservative addition to the existing structure. The decision bruised some feelings, and Ted was headed north to found his own community near Ithaca.

"I've got my own utopia to almost make," he said.

Each of the bedrooms in the guesthouse was named for a utopian novel. My roommate was the ex-con of our group, and our room was called Erewhon for the 1872 Samuel Butler novel. A small pamphlet, titled "Not Utopia Yet," had been left on each of our beds. It lowered expectations for the visitor program and detailed the joining process. After the visitor period ended, the community took a vote: You could be accepted, rejected, or asked to visit for another three weeks.

I took a walk before the other visitors arrived. Twin Oaks was part farm, part summer camp. The community grew its own vegetables on neatly planted acres, and dairy cows wandered broad fields between twice-daily milkings. Nature paths lat-

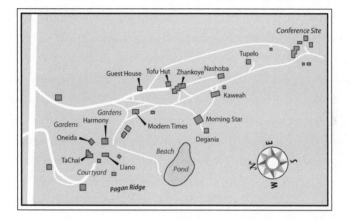

ticed surrounding forests managed with an eye to a range of bird species that would have impressed Aristophanes.

The population stood at just under one hundred, with about a dozen children and adults ranging in age from early twenties to mideighties. The land had originally been a tobacco farm, and over the years the community had added several hundred acres and two dozen buildings as it grew. The structures stretched south from the courtyard for half a mile: a dairy barn, an auto shop, a meeting hall, a warehouse complex, and a handful of residences that provided each member with one hundred square feet of personal space. Most of the buildings were named for communal experiments of the past: Harmony and Oneida stood on the courtyard along with Tachai (a community work brigade under Mao) and Llano (a twentieth-century socialist commune in California). Twin Oaks thought of itself as a village. The courtyard was downtown, and other residences represented facets of society: Kaweah (another short-lived socialist experiment) was the child-friendly suburbs; Nashoba (an Owenite community in Tennessee) was the retirement home favored by older members; and Tupelo (a rare tree) was the party house for younger members, a fraternity for anarchists.

Just up from the visitor house was the Tofu Hut, which produced sixteen hundred pounds of tofu per day. It was immaculate on the inside but looked something like an old fishing trawler on the outside, and the weathered, half-finished look held true for most Twin Oaks buildings. The main commissary stood a few steps farther up the path, and was called ZK, short for Zhankoye, a pre-Zionist community in Russia. ZK was Grand Central, and here most members took cafeteria-style meals twice per day, lunch and dinner, and conducted intracommunity communications via several primitive mailbox systems.

I headed for one of the smaller kitchens in Llano, where a few tables and a couch offered the feel of a tiny café. Nine months before, I'd come to Twin Oaks for my own Saturday tour. A member named Ezra—a blond Elvis who almost always looked as though he'd just woken from a nap—had walked several guests through the community, telling stories and emphasizing that the central value at Twin Oaks these days had nothing to do with B. F. Skinner—it was egalitarianism, gender equality. Since the eighties, Twin Oaks had been home to both an annual conference on intentional communities and another on feminism. For two weeks in August, a portion of the community was made off-limits to men. When Ezra's tour had come round to the kitchen in Llano, I spotted a box of group reading texts on a shelf: On top was a copy of *The Charlotte Perkins Gilman Reader.* It was from this—and the community's emphasis on feminism—that I had built my own theory on Twin Oaks.

37

Though Skinner claimed to have been inspired by his wife's domestic malaise, *Walden Two*, like *Looking Backward*, pretty much ignored women's rights. Even the skeptical Professor Burris is eventually seduced by a hastily drawn love interest. "Mrs. Olson" loves flowers and sewing.

Utopian novels generally fudge details to demonstrate the wisdom of sweeping ideologies. But just as Pleistocene Rewilding was a utopian movement attempting to undo the dystopian results of earlier utopias, so had a trickle of utopian novels written by women worked to undo the double standard embraced by utopians from Plato to Noyes to Bellamy to Skinner.

The authors of feminist utopias sometimes hid their work even from their husbands. Often only a name and a fanciful story have been handed down. Margaret Cavendish's *The Description of a New World, Called the Blazing World* (1666) is an early *Lord Jim* in which a young woman is accidentally brought to a city called Paradise and mistaken for a goddess. Sarah Scott's *A Description of Millennium Hall* (1762) fictionalizes a community of gentlewomen that was first suggested in Mary Astell's *A Serious Proposal to the Ladies* (1694). The protagonist of Mary Griffith's *Three Hundred Years Hence* (1836) is buried in an avalanche, pickles for three centuries, and wakes to discover a world of perfect equality.* And Mary Bradley Lane's *Mizora* (1880) features a young newlywed who sails off the end of the earth and discovers a land populated entirely by women—they have robots for domestic work, something like cell phones, and, as to men, the heroine is told, "We eliminated them."

Charlotte Perkins Gilman revisited the all-female civilization a couple of generations later. Known now almost exclusively for a single short story, "The Yellow Wall-Paper" (a feminist dystopia), Gilman was actually wildly prolific, and in 1915 she produced what has since become the most influential of feminist utopias, a work that was first serialized in *Forerunner,* a magazine that Gilman wrote entirely herself and sold for one dollar per copy. In *Forerunner*'s seven-year run, Gilman published twenty-eight books' worth of material.

Her utopia was later compiled into two separate volumes, *Herland* and *With Her in Ourland*. She offered the standard formula in triplicate: Three male adventurers stumble onto an all-female country of three million inhabitants, hidden in the far north. The romance Gilman assigns to each of her protagonists (one ends in rape, another in marriage, another in vibrant intellectual partnership) critiqued gender relations of the time.

"*Herland* is a very funny book," said a later critic.

"I wrote it to preach," Gilman said. "If it is literature, that just happened."

---

* I find it impossible not to note that the plot of Bellamy's *Looking Backward* matches Griffith's almost verbatim, fifty years later. Toward the end of *Three Hundred Years Hence*, Griffith opines: "But if you will only *look back* you will perceive that in every benevolent scheme . . . it was women's influence that promoted and fostered it." (italics mine)

The Charlotte Perkins Gilman Reader included sections from both novels. My theory was that Twin Oaks had managed to endure where so many others failed by shifting its focus from Skinner to Gilman and a new wave of feminist utopian novels that crested in the early 1970s, just as the community was putting its feet on the ground. But when I returned to Llano's café on the first day of my visitor period, I found *The Charlotte Perkins Gilman Reader* still there. It didn't look like anyone had touched it in all the nine months I'd been gone.

38

On the fourth day of our visitor period, lunch on the patio outside ZK was disrupted when someone noticed two black snakes copulating on the side of a tree. A crowd wandered over to observe the slick forms clinging impossibly to the bark, the male's raw pink penis prying up its scales. The scene became spectacle, but no one tied the obvious threads: sex, tree, snake, paradise.

The next evening I wandered down to the courtyard with the scholar and the ex-con to sit with a group of members watching another group of members try their hand at the hula hoop. Twin Oaks deemphasized competition in play, and some of the women of the community had turned the hula hoop into an apparatus for something approaching a veil dance. We were not there long before a prominent member, a man named Pax, sat down with us.

Pax was Twin Oaks's Peter Pan. He bragged that he was three days older than Osama bin Laden, but he might have passed for thirty-two. He was part of the community's polyamorous marriage, which stood then at three spouses and a child, but he had girlfriends in Portland as well. An anarchist with a heavy-lidded leer, Pax was well-known in the world of intentional communities for revolutionary fervor and an ability to navigate complicated romance. He had a manic charisma, a talent for storytelling, and an inexplicable history of working for a defense contractor. He had changed his name to Paxus Calta from Earl Flansburgh. His father was a famous architect, his brother was a rock star. He had been Quill and Dagger at Cornell, but graduate school soured him. "I fell in love with a witch, got mixed up with the anarchists, and it was all downhill from there," he told me later. He became a gypsy activist, wandering Europe to protest nuclear power, and now he had lived at Twin Oaks for a decade and would have been its leader long ago if not for the community's strong anti-authoritarian streak. The people who were voted onto the "planner board"—the government proposed in *Walden Two*—tended to be those who accepted the role reluctantly.

Pax explained that one of his jobs at Twin Oaks was managing the "propaganda campaign" waged to get word out about the community.

"What do you mean by propaganda?"

"Outreach." He shrugged. "You know, the media, the reporters, when they come here and ask us if this is utopia yet, we say, 'No, but we can see it from here.'" He gestured off to the hula hoopers. "It looks like that."

39

I agreed.

It took a little while to get used to the farm's humming stasis, and I made three trips to the pond before I mustered the courage to skinny-dip, but from there it was easy to slide into the community's peaceful routine. In the mornings I walked to the kitchen in Llano for homemade granola and to read while members wandered in and out, preparing for days at the warehouse or a shift in the Tofu Hut. What Twin Oakers called "the mainstream" began to feel remote, and not just because of the social norms of our SLG. The community subscribed to *Bitch* but not *The New York Times*. There were no televisions and just a few old computers with Internet access. A neo-Luddite sentiment prevailed. Morning showers began to seem like a needless luxury, and I developed a Napoleonic appreciation of body odor. In the afternoons I cut myself big chunks of raw-milk cheese that the community had in abundance and took plates of it to a hammock to nap, read, or listen to someone fiddle on a guitar or musical saw. Once I made a flute of my cupped hands and blew a call to a pigeon on top of Harmony. For a moment it was fooled and answered.

I met a member who was reading Marge Piercy's *Woman on the Edge of Time*, which was one of that surge of seventies' feminist utopias along with novels by Dorothy Bryant, Joanna Russ, and Ursula K. LeGuin. But the member was alone in her reading—my theory was ruined. *Herland* had not appeared in book form until 1979, anyway. Gilman's popularity faded dramatically after she took her own life in 1935.

"I have preferred chloroform to cancer," she wrote, in the pages of an autobiography that didn't sell.

The first I heard of Kat Kinkade at Twin Oaks was a rumor that she had cancer, too. She had a year to live and would be returning to the community so that they could care for her. She would receive visitors at Nashoba on Sunday afternoons. Visits were creditable labor.

A sizable portion of our first week's labor quota was filled by meetings.

Coyote, a shaggy ex-professor of creative writing, introduced us to the labor credit system, which he described as "sheer fucking genius." Members self-recorded hours on "labor sheets," and any hours worked over quota became PSCs (personal service credits), a unit of currency members could use to purchase goods from one another. Pax's wife Hawina, a feral elf, lectured us on membership. The community's rate of acceptance was high, she said, but so was turnover. Twin Oaks's ur-father, Keenan, detailed policies on children and government, the former visibly disturbing a few of our group. If a couple wished to have a child, they submitted an application. They could be rejected either because the community's ratio of workers to dependents was skewed or because the community didn't feel they were ready to be parents.

The child policy at Twin Oaks had come from Skinner as well. Skinner, in turn, had borrowed from two sources: Oneida, which had passed dozens of children through a communal child-rearing program, and the kibbutzim of Israel, which had been imported from Russia and were themselves inspired by a version of Fourier that had spread east rather than west.* In its early years Twin Oaks had devoted a building to its own communal child-rearing

---

* Like Hawthorne, Dostoyevsky had mocked Fourierism in an 1865 short story, though he had once stood before a firing squad for having adhered to a Fourier movement.

effort, taking a stab at conditioning techniques that Skinner had described but vaguely. They called the building Degania, after the first of hundreds of kibbutzim in Israel. Degania Alef was founded in 1910, and the kibbutzim had flourished for many years. But the early socialism eventually faded, and Degania Alef was also the last kibbutz. A month before the start of our visitor period, it announced it was privatizing.

Twin Oaks's communal child-rearing program never really worked. Keenan told stories of days when parents had little say over their children because procreative capability was not assumed to be a qualification for child care. If you traveled off the farm with your biological child, Keenan said, a qualified professional traveled along with you.

"Oh, God," the ex-con of our group said.

"I *know*," Keenan said.

We had gathered in Kaweah for the meeting. Kaweah might have been just about any starter home in Utopia Road, its great room off the kitchen strewn with toys and children's books. The children in question wandered in and out as Keenan spoke. They regarded all this utopia stuff as nonsense. The community had produced two notable children: a singer-songwriter with a few recorded collections and a young man who had left the farm for a time, only to return and marry Pax and Hawina.

When Keenan turned to Twin Oaks's government, the scholar was forced to reconsider his hypothesis that Twin Oaks was a labor dictatorship. It turned out that any decision the planners made—and they controlled cash reserves of more than a million dollars—could be overruled by a simple majority of the community. Anyone could call for a vote.

"It's classic communism," Keenan said.

"Well," the scholar said, "Marx would call it primitive communism."

"We're *trying* to be a *more evolved* communism."

"No, no, no! You *want* to be primitive."

41

It was said that people joined the community not for ideology but because they wanted to fall in love. Sure enough, our visitor group began to pair off. The ex-clown started spending a lot of time with the ex-con, and the former acrobat headed to the philosophy student's room at night. The would-be Fulbright took her lunches with a mountain man member named Bucket, and the innocent girl-child was soon significantly less innocent. A number of people seemed implicated. Once she walked up to me, looked me in the eye, and unfastened one button of my shirt before walking away.

"Hormones," said the divorcée, who hadn't found anyone herself. A few days later she left the community.

After a week I was significantly missing the significant adjacent cohabitator. I sneaked her e-mails: ". . . missing you much . . . ," ". . . thinking of you all the time . . . ," etc. As well, I craved a drink. Drugs of any kind were rare in a community where everyone billed out at two dollars per day, but I heard Coyote kept a stash. One morning I stopped him as he was zipping along from ZK to the courtyard in one of the golf carts the community provided for older members. I made small talk about the Kenneth Patchen book he was carrying, and he invited me to his room in Tachai that afternoon.

Coyote's beard was identical to the hair on his head, which made him look like a large puppet. His room was a shrine to Beat poetry. Books stuffed shelves on one cramped wall; others displayed hookahs, wilting flowers, tchotchkes, liquor. The low ceiling was the floor of the loft that doubled his square footage. Coyote had been thrown out of academia twice. He had lived in the room for fifteen years.

"Do you want some gin laced with pot?"

"Yes."

He produced a square glass flask filled with "jungle juice," a bottom-shelf medley with an herbal sting. Among the clutter of the room—statues of rhinos and portraits of himself commissioned from other members and paid for with PSCs—I noticed a doll, a bearded man, anatomically correct.

"Is that Ginsberg?"

"No, it's me."

He bragged that the doll was accurate—he had the smallest dick in the world. He took it along when he traveled and had photos of the naked imp posed among the dead soldiers of drinking battles long past. Coyote claimed that a member named Thomas had once kissed Ginsberg on the mouth, so Coyote had kissed Thomas on the mouth in turn. He had similarly oblique connections to Raymond Carver (picked him up hitchhiking), Kurt Vonnegut (distant relation), and Wendell Berry (sent Coyote a poem with one typo). Coyote had once produced six chapters of a novel "faster than Kerouac wrote *On the Road*," and sent them to an agent. Then he panicked. "Those six chapters? I burned them. *Fuck*." But it wasn't as though he didn't have material out there. He'd once sent some work to a friend employed at City Lights Bookstore. It wound up in Ferlinghetti's hands. "My greatest line? He *used* it. 'This is the first day of the rest of your life.' *My* line."

Coyote pumped his fist whenever he thought truth had been achieved in the abstract. And he had a habit, even when smoking his pipe, of selling his own one-liners with a pantomime of hitting a bud, as though his jokes were funnier if you imagined having been high when you heard them.

I asked to borrow E. M. Cioran's *History and Utopia*, which Coyote had on a shelf because Jim Harrison had once mentioned Cioran in a novella. I'd been thinking about Cioran at Twin Oaks because he'd once said that people should change their names whenever something important happened to them. Coyote had underscored a passage in the first chapter.

> If a man has not, by the time he is thirty, yielded to the fascination of every form of extremism—I don't know whether he is to be admired or scorned, regarded as a saint or a corpse.

42

Our visitor period would end just as Twin Oaks celebrated its fortieth anniversary.

Coyote passed the jungle juice and claimed the community was headed for another golden age. A few years back they had been thrown into a tailspin when the main distributor of their hammocks suddenly cut off a quarter-century-old standing order. Twin Oaks's economy crashed, the population dipped to around sixty, and members now spoke of an era of living "in austerity" as though it was an unfortunate country they'd all been forced to visit. The tofu business had been an effort at diversification, and the schism over its expansion amounted to more than just a debate over a business decision.

Philosophically, the hammock business had always been a double-edged proposition. Members weren't keen on producing durable goods for the leisure class, but the hammock shop had become a social space where bonds formed across the weaving jigs. Tofu was the opposite dilemma: It appealed as a product and generated repeat customers, but the work was loud and difficult, and they still hadn't figured out how to dispose of the waste responsibly. Just a few days after our visitor group arrived, the decision to expand tofu was complicated by the first correspondence from the hammock distributor in several years: They wanted six thousand units for the following spring. The community was buzzing with opinions as to whether they should accept the order, and beneath the tallies of hours and dollars was a low-frequency discussion of what kind of community they would become.

There were brewing social crises, too. Shifting values had caused a number of long-term members to schedule their departures. As well, the community was embroiled in its first expulsion process in a decade and a half. A member who went by the name Bok Choy had been accused of padding hours on her labor sheet, taking sick time after party nights. We'd been told that Twin Oaks generally handled difficult personalities by conspiring against them—members would approach at intervals and tell troublemakers to go away, they weren't wanted.

It usually worked, but not with Bok Choy, who now knocked on Coyote's door. His room was a common meeting place for those looking to take the edge off.

Bok Choy had a punky, dyed haircut and a peculiar glare. She wore a T-shirt with the words "Math Masters" and the four basic symbols of arithmetic printed on the front.

"Were you on a math team?" I asked.

"No, it's a secret society."

"Really?"

"I can't say much more."

"Okay!"

She was here for counseling, the office hours of Coyote's hipster English teacher persona. They chatted for a while about the nature of the universe, matter, time, and space, and then Bok Choy offered a reverie on the quality of person to be found, these days, in insane asylums. She was considering her options. If she left Twin Oaks, she suggested, she could stage a manic episode out in the mainstream and land in a hospital somewhere. This appealed to the Kesey in Coyote.

"Oh, yeah! If I could get locked up in one of those places when I was old and couldn't find any other gig—I could get *real* cozy."

Coyote was confident the community would come out stronger on the other side of all its crises, but members almost uniformly believed that the days leading up to the fortieth anniversary were charged with change and stress. As an outsider accustomed to a hectic world, I had difficulty sensing the subtle dramas playing out. Maybe it was the jungle juice, but as other members arrived and crammed into Coyote's room, nine of us passing pipes and bottles, it didn't feel like a place about to un-

dergo revolution. Rather, it felt as though the revolution had already been achieved—the dirty work was done, the necessary
heads were in baskets—and it was time to laugh and smoke and
rest. I hadn't come to Twin Oaks to join, but now that my theory
had been foiled the thought came creeping in that I could leave
behind my experiment, leave behind my life, and maybe even
call the cohabitator and invite her along. Twin Oaks was not on
the brink of a golden age; it *was* utopia. It *was* possible to shed
your name, it *was* possible to shed the idea of money and private
property. A better world *could* be made intentionally, and stress
and change only meant that you were eternally vigilant to how
even small decisions generated long-term impacts. You didn't
have to cop an ironic pose to endure the nasty mess of the mainstream. You didn't have to read a hopeful novel about an impossible place to escape where you actually lived. You didn't have to
tell a joke to laugh with joy.

The feeling continued into evening, when the community
split into three groups. Some members climbed up to the woods
on Pagan Ridge for a women-only ritual. A number of men gathered on another part of the farm. And a mixed-gender group of
us met at the pond beneath the full moon to strip and swim. The
air shimmered with fireflies. The water was as hot as a body, but
chilly pockets over deep spots tickled my scrotum. A few of us
treaded water in the middle of the pool, musing on the identity
of a very bright star overhead.

"It's Venus," someone corrected us.

The scholar did naked back flips off a floating platform
in the middle of the pond until someone told him there was
a cement block in the water nearby, and he'd better knock
it off. I kicked my way over to see how his hypothesis was

coming along. He had decided Twin Oaks was a republic after all.

"So do you think it's utopia?"

He smiled. "Well, most visions of utopia start with a complete change in psychology. I don't see that happening here."

43

Cioran wrote: "In the long run, life without utopia is suffocating, for the multitude at least: threatened otherwise with petrifaction, the world must have a new madness."

Then he called Fourier's phalansteries "the most effective vomitive I know."

44

"Skinner" was almost a bad word at Twin Oaks. It was still possible to find older members who had joined the community precisely because of its *Walden Two* ambitions, but it wasn't wise to go around citing Skinner openly.

On Sunday I sat down for lunch with a woman named Piper. She was eighty-two, and had been at Twin Oaks for thirty years. People said she was ornery, but I'd also heard that she was anxious to recruit disciples to help her with a process that she had invented to teach local children to read. The system, she told me, offered rewards for effort rather than success.

"Like a token economy?"

"Yes. I tell them, touch your head. They touch their heads. I tell them, touch your leg. They touch their legs. Then I tell them, touch the ceiling—and they jump as high as they can."

"Sounds like Skinner," I tried.

"That's right." She took a new look at me. "There are so many people I can't even say that name to."

"You're okay with behaviorism."

"We could use a little more of it around here. Now, let me eat. But tell me: How is it you're so conversant with B. F. Skinner?"

I told her I'd read *Walden Two* but didn't mention that I'd looked up Skinner's critics as well. In the sixties, interest in the novel on the fringe had been matched or bested by anxiety over behaviorism in the mainstream. Arthur Koestler derided behaviorism as a "heroic shortcut from the rat in the box to the human condition," and Noam Chomsky claimed it was "as congenial to the libertarian as to the fascist." Carl Rogers, professor of "unconditional positive regard," took the gentler approach one might expect, but concluded that Skinner had made "a serious underestimation of the problem of power."

Piper looked up when I said I'd read *Beyond Freedom and Dignity* as well.

"Now that book," she said, pointing her fork tines at me, "it's a shame that one didn't get more attention."

"It was a bestseller."

"Only for a little while."

"Skinner was on the cover of *Time*," I said. The article, "Skinner's Utopia: Panacea, or Path to Hell?," described *Beyond Freedom and Dignity* as a nonfiction version of *Walden Two*. "What more could you ask for?"

Piper's stare explained her reputation. "No more questions. Now let me eat my lunch."

In the afternoon I took the path up to Nashoba to meet Kinkade.

Nashoba had a grandmotherly atmosphere and was tidier than the rest of the community. Apart from the care team that received labor credits for looking out for her, Kinkade was alone in the house. She sat in a corner, a small and shrinking woman sunk into an overstuffed chair. She wore a flowered top and a green skirt spread over legs that had begun to betray her. Nylons throttled her calves.

"Are you the man who wanted to meet me?"

"Yes."

She couldn't hear well, and I pulled a chair over to sit close. We chatted about Skinner. She had done transcription for him during the years she'd lived in Boston and recalled a time when he'd become enraged when she missed a page. She had hoped to interact with him intellectually, but he wasn't interested. The truth was, Skinner's wife would never have allowed him to join a community himself. Of Twin Oaks, Kinkade said, he was most interested in rumors of group massages.

I asked what he had suggested as a moneymaking enterprise.

"There wasn't anything. We were pioneers in that."

"So he was—"

"Naïve. He didn't know what he was talking about."

"Did you ever tell him that?"

"No. He was too busy talking about sex."

"Did you like him?"

"I liked him," she said. "But I didn't enjoy him."

She had never heard of Charlotte Perkins Gilman or *Herland*, but she had read one of the later Gilman knockoffs, Sheri S. Tepper's *The Gate to Women's Country*. Work was the real problem of utopias, she said, and *Looking Backward* had solved that. She described Bellamy's "industrial army" as slave labor.

"This isn't *Walden Two*. It never was. It's Twin Oaks. We had to work with the people we had—and we had the hippies." The hippies had regarded Kinkade much in the same way *Walden Two*'s Frazier was regarded by his antagonists, and even now Kinkade wasn't particularly revered by the membership. "I lusted after the plannership," she admitted, "but people were afraid of me. They thought I just wanted power. But I wanted power so I could *get things done*. I *liked* the job. But people were afraid."

I suggested Twin Oaks had achieved something moving much more slowly than what Skinner had envisioned, but Kinkade was skeptical that community was the long-term answer.

"How can people from different places get along? Here, this is fine, we have people from all over the country, of a fairly singular mind-set—and they can't get along. And then you have China and India, Indonesia—to say nothing of Africa. What can you do to bring them together?"

When I got up to leave, Kinkade asked for my last name. It was the first time in more than a week that I'd uttered it. She looked me head to toe, and some of the Twin Oaks sexual tension that Skinner had been so curious about seemed to have rubbed off on her. It was still there, tired but alive.

"So are you considering joining?"

"Yes."

"Really?"

One of her caregivers scolded her for the implication.

"No," she said. "I mean it in a good way. I might have to come back." Her eyes held mine. "Here's someone who's not tired of talking about things. Freedom. Liberty."

46

Our labor quota rose in our second and third weeks. We spent long hours picking rhubarb, peeling garlic, tying knots in the polypropylene rope the community used for its hammocks, power washing the Tofu Hut. In addition to recruiting members, the visitor program was the community's industrial army. Visitor hours filled out the time budgets. In the community's arcane reckoning, our labor was "free."

One morning a member named Woody walked into the Llano kitchen with a headless chicken. Woody was the closest thing the community had to a real Thoreau. A documentary film had been made about a log cabin Woody had built by himself in Canada. He knew how to do everything—from designing Web pages to handcrafting wooden turtles with secret compartments in their shells—and he had taught himself all of it. Woody represented a distinctly antifeminist streak in the community: Of concern to some members was a peculiar image he had photoshopped for his computer's desktop, a nude snapshot of one of the female members with added dragonfly wings that turned her into a fairy.

Woody was in charge of the slaughter of livestock, but he hadn't slaughtered the chicken. A raccoon had. It had sliced the bird's gullet and yanked the sheath of its skin over its head like the hood of a jacket. The raccoon ate most of its neck, but the chicken was still alive when Woody found it.

"I had to do a cesarean section," he said, holding up the bird's last perfect egg. "The mother didn't survive."

A member named McCune sat nearby with some newspapers the community had inherited from a neighbor. McCune had been at Twin Oaks longer than anyone except Kinkade, and I'd been hoping to run into him because he'd been present when Skinner had made his one and only visit to the community. McCune had tousled hair, a patchy beard, and a reputation for avoiding friendships with new members until they'd stuck around for a couple of years.

I asked about Skinner.

"I didn't interact with him. I saw him, didn't speak with him. I'm sure he got a tour, answered some questions." McCune found something interesting picking through the newspapers. "Look, June 1. Not bad."

It was only five days old. He went back to his reading. A moment later, six topless women entered the kitchen, hot and dirty and tired, taking a break from the morning garden shift. McCune didn't look up.

47

I worked the next morning's garden shift with some of the same women. The peas were growing faster than the community could eat or pick them. We spent an hour there, then weeded tomatoes with mattocks and hula hoes. It was hard, dirty labor. Halfway through the shift, one of the women caught the scent of the chestnut tree over near the visitor house.

"Disgusting."

"I kind of like it," another woman said.

"What's wrong with chestnuts?" I said.

"It smells like cum."

I had long since replaced showering with swimming entirely. After the tomatoes I headed for a little beach by the pond with plastic lounge chairs and towels. Hawina followed me down.

Hawina was somewhere between fifteen and fifty years of age—you couldn't be more specific than that. She had the heady, fecund air of a bog. She finished all her meals by licking her plate and using the ends of her hair as dental floss. I'd heard a rumor that Hawina had given the scholar a hard time at his membership interview. It turned out the scholar was rethinking a professorship he'd been offered in Colorado and was seriously considering Twin Oaks. Part of the joining process included an interview in which you were asked about your history of STDs and incarcerations. Then you were offered a frank assessment of your chances. In mine I'd been told that I looked "promising" but seemed to be "something of a loner." Apparently, Hawina had confronted the scholar over his tendency to present himself as more knowledgeable about communities than those who had been at it for decades.

She stripped and waded into the pond behind me. I kicked slowly out toward the middle while Hawina dove beneath the surface and tried to swim the pool's breadth underwater. Her body showed luminous through the murk, each stroke squirting her gently forward, like a squid. She surfaced close to me once, slicking back her hair.

"I thought I was going to touch you!"

We climbed to the chairs on the beach to dry. It was hard not to sneak glances at Hawina as we chatted. I could imagine no good reason why the mainstream had denied itself the intricate pleasure of the sun's warmth on genitals.

Hawina said her relationship was falling apart—then corrected herself. "I guess I should say *one* of my relationships."

I wondered if she meant Pax. A German journalist who had recently written a story about Twin Oaks had returned to the community for the anniversary, and earlier I had seen her walking with Pax through the courtyard holding hands. Outreach.

"Could be worse," I said, thinking of Hawina's other husband and son.

"It's hard to imagine. But yes, it could."

I went to Coyote's room to return the Cioran. I was hoping for jungle juice. I'd become a regular. There were no days off at Twin Oaks, just your forty-two hours, some of which was assigned and some of which you had to hunt down for yourself. It was easy to fall behind, and I had begun to think of everything—making the bed, exercise—in terms of creditable labor. Six hours per day was already wearying. Coyote's was a respite.

"I'm a liar," he was saying when I walked in. "I lie."

A few others had beaten me there, and Coyote was going through a routine I'd already heard. He had made himself who he was by repeating stories and speeches to new groups of visitors each month.

"I'm a goddamned magician! What I do is get you looking at one hand, and then I do something else with this one over here."

He began to fix his pipe. I spotted one of Woody's wooden turtles, with its secret compartment, tucked away on a shelf.

"Maybe you should keep your stash in there."

Coyote smiled. "I'd need a bigger turtle."

48

I showered and shaved at the guesthouse before I went to see Kinkade again.

The other visitors were taking the afternoon off and had gathered in the living room to gossip about the farm's many budding romances. Members were finding their way to one another, and even the scholar had been seen strolling at dusk with a curly-haired member named Trina.

"When you're gone we're going to gossip about *you*," the former acrobat told me.

"Good luck."

"He loves Kat Kinkade!"

Kinkade was not alone this time. A number of members had tagged along with the German journalist for a visit. The journalist had brought a photographer, who was crawling around on the floor to get a good angle on Kinkade in her chair. I edged in close again.

"I heard you had a good result." A rumor of an encouraging scan had shot through the community, though Kinkade's prognosis was the same.

"You heard that?" She looked out at the room. "Looks like I'm community property!"

The room wasn't listening. The German journalist was describing her article to a few members, answering questions about when it might appear, and some other members had wandered over to the kitchen for snacks and more gossip. The photographer was still snapping pictures.

"I'm no hero," Kinkade told me. She turned to the photographer but gestured toward me. "Do you really need so many pictures of me? He's more attractive."

The photographer smiled and kept snapping.

Kinkade touched my arm. "I embarrassed you. Are you *really* considering joining?"

"I'm thinking about it."

"Well. *I'd* be very attracted to the idea of your membership."

49

By the third week, the significant adjacent cohabitator was convinced I was not coming home. I was still sneaking her messages ("...you're always in my thoughts...," "...no, I don't really want to join..."), and on our final week's labor schedule I finagled a day when I could ride along into town on a supply trip. I would meet the cohabitator for a quick visit.

I wasn't entirely at home back in the mainstream. I was struck by the effusive apology of a man in a bookstore who merely brushed my elbow, and a cup of coffee and the chill of a café's air-conditioning made me higher than the jungle juice ever had. Still, I had begun to grow tired of labor sheets and garden work. I bought a copy of *Herland* for Kinkade and a cheap tequila for Coyote.

The cohabitator found me waiting at an outside table. She reached out to me at once—to button my shirt.

"This utopia needs work," I said.

"The work *is* the utopia," she corrected me.

50

Two days before the anniversary I ducked under an electric cow fence and crossed a stream to find the site where Kinkade would be interred when the time came.* The community had had several deaths, and on the land's highest point a few cleared paths wound between oblong mounds. A crucifix marked one, a Buddha squatted on another. There was a hammock here as well, and I lay in it for a while trying to hit a trance state. The council of birds was endless. I opened my eyes to several insects searching my chest for a cavity, a point of entry.

About a hundred former members attended the anniversary celebration. A contra dance celebrated community spirit, and a crowd jammed into the living room in Tachai for a slide show of early photos. There was a talent show in the courtyard and a performance of a play written for the occasion. I stopped by Coyote's to say good-bye. He went to sleep every day at 6:00 P.M., and the anniversary would be no exception. He was sitting with a member named David, a man who'd had some trouble with the law in the sixties and had been bouncing among communities ever since.

Coyote was pleased with the tequila.

"So you really joining? I been thinking you were just blowing through—decided we were too fuckin' crazy."

"What's wrong with crazy?"

* Kinkade died in 2008.

"Nothing. Not a thing. So you'll be here?"

"You have to vote. We'll see."

He shook his head. "It's like I told you, with this place. You got to check your idealism at the door. This is just like living anywhere else on the planet."

David chuckled. "Coyote, it sounds like you're trying to talk him out of it."

"Maybe I am!" He hit his pipe and looked at me. "It's interesting, this place. But there's a bigger place outside of it. A guy like you can find a home in it."

51

Near the end of *Walden Two*, Frazier and Burris hike up to the community's highest point, a ridge called the Throne, to survey utopia.

"I look upon my work, and behold, it is good," Frazier says.

In the theological debate that ensues, Frazier allows that his world isn't perfect but insists that he is disappointed by his creation far less often than God in the Old Testament.

Yet Skinner was disappointed by Twin Oaks.

"Kat and her friends simply muddled through," he later wrote.

52

When dark fell on the celebration the community pulled out a projector to show a film of Skinner's visit to Twin Oaks. The trip had been arranged by a television documentary crew. The old show was thrown up onto the wall of Modern Times, a building named for a short-lived community on Long Island. Skinner had wandered through the fledgling commune in a bad plaid suit, and now an apotheosized version of him, twelve feet high, repeated the trip, his image illuminating peppers we'd planted two weeks before. The members mostly chuckled at their old foolishness as Skinner offered poor advice to communards who even then knew more about community life than he ever had.

When it was over I walked through the dissolving party to Nashoba. I ran into one of Kinkade's caregivers along the way. She was asleep, the member said, but I should wake her and make sure she drank some water. Inside, Kinkade's head tipped to her shoulder. I touched her arm.

"Kat?"

She came to and smiled.

"How are you?" I said.

"I'm okay."

"I brought you a present."

"You did?"

"How do you feel?"

"I'm cold."

I fetched a throw from the couch and tucked it around her shoulders and thighs. She drank from the glass by her side.

"That's nice," she said.

I gave her *Herland*. She promised to read it.

We talked about the decision the community had made to modestly expand the tofu business. It was an example, Kinkade said, of a tension between growth and security that underwrote all decision making at Twin Oaks. The community had not built a new structure in a number of years, but she remembered when they were putting up new buildings regularly. They would start a new residence before old ones were even finished. Finally, a number of members became dissatisfied with homes half complete. A decision was made to slow growth.

"That was pretty much the end for me," Kinkade said. "I didn't come here to finish buildings! Pah! I came to grow. I wanted to be—important. So that was the end. I offered myself as the first member of a new community, but it was a terrible mistake. I should have stayed and finished the buildings."

I asked her how the community had managed to survive, after all.

"We never believed in behaviorism in any serious way. We gave it a year or two of loyalty. After that, various ideas tried to be our central goal, but none succeeded. I may have had something to do with that. I was always there, arguing common sense, practical selfishness, and utopian idealism. I wouldn't go away. But perhaps I take too much credit. My dreams were based on Skinner and Bellamy. They took for granted thoroughgoing equality and work toward communitywide happiness. Twin Oaks is as close as I could come."

53

Ten days after the anniversary I was admitted to Twin Oaks. I sent brief regrets. The scholar was rejected but invited to visit again—so they could get to know him a little better.

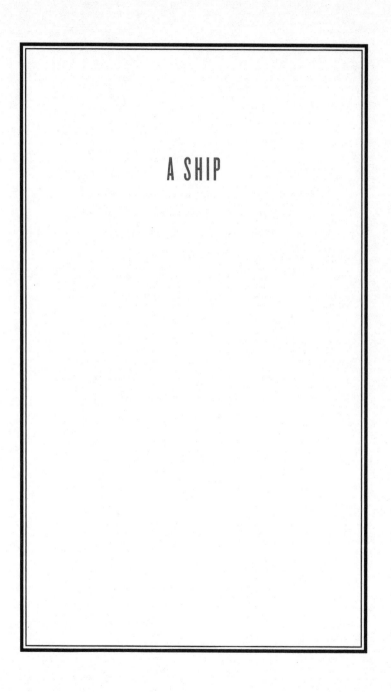

A SHIP

*It is clear that if there is to be any revival of
the utopian imagination in the near future,
it cannot return to the old-style spatial
utopias. New utopias would have to derive
their form from the shifting and dissolving
movement of society that is gradually
replacing the fixed locations of life.*
—NORTHROP FRYE,
"Varieties of Literary Utopias"

*Nowadays we do not resist and overcome
the great stream of things, but rather float
upon it. We build now not citadels,
but ships of state.*
—H. G. WELLS,
A Modern Utopia

At the start of William Alexander Taylor's 1901 utopian novel *Intermere* a small steamship runs into a fog bank three days north of the equator and drifts into a whirlpool. "I felt myself being dragged down into the immeasurable watery depths," the hero recounts. He loses consciousness—and promptly wakes in a hammock on the curved deck of an entirely different kind of vessel, one with a "succession of suites and apartments, richly but artistically furnished." The hero imagines for a moment that he is already in Paradise, but the ship, a "merocar," turns out to be just one advance in a perfect world hidden inside the earth.

The jump from steam-powered transport to luxury yacht places *Intermere* midway along an evolution in utopian thought: A range of authors, architects, and engineers first identified paradise as a floating island, then as an island accessible by ship, and finally as the ship itself. Transport became destination.

In 2002, when the unique vessel *The World* of ResidenSea shoved off from an Oslo wharf—christened by a triumvirate of Norwegian priests with a cocktail of holy water and champagne—it marked the first time it was possible to own real estate onboard a ship.

The launch was greeted with telling fanfares.

"A global village at sea," said *The Boston Globe.*

"Utopia afloat," said *Maclean's.*

I flew to Norway to meet the man who had coaxed utopian ships off the drawing board. Knut Kloster Jr. met me at the airport, wearing, like Raphael Hythloday, a sea captain's cap low on his brow so I could recognize him. It was odd to be met by Kloster himself. He was the father of the modern cruise industry, the visionary scion of one of Norway's oldest shipping families.

"I'm glad I don't have to wear this hat anymore," Kloster said.

On the drive into Oslo, he felt obliged to point out the city's new high-speed train, and for the next couple days he would sustain that act of reluctant tour guide. The traffic downtown unnerved me. Kloster was almost eighty, but he was a large, buoyant, alert man, and he sluiced smartly through the streets, mumbling recriminations at drivers who didn't quite grasp the system of signalless intersections. We settled on the lobby of my hotel to begin our discussions. Almost all my discussions with Kloster would be about what we would discuss in the event that we decided, collectively, that his was a story worth telling. I liked him immensely.

Kloster didn't have a high regard for consistency, and even in our first chat he turned on a dime.

"Of course it's an interesting story," he said, of the grand megaship scheme he had first proposed in the 1970s. This wasn't *The World*. It was a plan originally code-named Phoenix Project, and over the years Kloster had spent tens of millions of dollars on it.

Then, in the very next moment, he said, "I'm a failure. I failed. You won't get whatever you're looking for from me. I'm not interested in cruise ships anymore."

He took me to the only park in Oslo where he could walk his German shepherd off leash, a sculpture garden filled with pieces by Gustav Vigeland. We climbed together to the center-piece, *Monolith Plateau,* which featured a huge granite column of piled and twisting bodies, people helping one another, straining against one another.

"It's about life," Kloster said. "Do you want to take a picture?"

"I don't have a camera."

"Good." He was terribly relieved. "I thought you would want me to take pictures."

Families and youths gathered around the statue, adding to the collage of forms.

"It's about life," Kloster said again.

56

Utopian literature is so full of ships and shipwrecks no book about utopia would be complete without the story of a voyage.

My voyage began when a delivery man ignored the threshold of my screen door and left a box in my foyer. I discovered the trespass with a little jolt of fear. Inside the box was another box, wrapped like a present with gold twine. Inside that was a leather document wallet stamped with a curious, round symbol—a porthole view of what looked like a setting sun. And inside the wallet was my invitation to *The World.*

I met the boat in Luleå, Sweden, on the Gulf of Bothnia. The town was not exactly a tourist destination, and the only word my taxi driver needed by way of address was "ship." At any given moment *The World* might have a population of 200 souls and 250 crew, giving it a unique passenger-to-staff ratio. Except there were no passengers, really. Apartments on *The World* ranged in price from $1 million to $8 million, and many of the residents used the ship as a second home—or third, or fourth. *The World* circled the globe endlessly, following world events and stopping at ports most cruise ships ignored. Like Luleå. Thus, it sometimes accepted humble moorings, and was now docked just up the coast from town, past some broken-down railroads and in line with a barnacly icebreaker named *Twin Screws* for its propellers.

The taxi passed through the ship's cyclone-fence checkpoint—manned by members of its Gurkha-recruited security force. I hurried up the gangway because it was raining.

A crowd of residents huddled inside, pressed together in the ship's onboard security lock, waiting to disembark. I'd been told that privacy was the ship's highest priority, but the residents looked friendly enough, bright and cheery, though not like tourists, and with a glow to them. The glow of knowing your time belonged to you.

When I stepped onboard one of the bright, cheery women recognized the trope of the moment. "We're the welcoming committee!" she said.

Which was a joke, because she was obviously not a professional welcomer. I was in her way, and they were all headed for my taxi to explore Luleå for the day.

57

Plato's Atlantis, home to a "wonderful empire" that no man can visit for "ships and voyages were not as yet," implies having floated on the surface of the ocean by sinking beneath it—like a ship.

Callimachus the librarian describes Delos, birthplace of Apollo, as "a tiny island wandering over the seas."

Lucian's *True History* satirizes a Greek tendency toward exaggeration, poking fun at Jason and the Argonauts. Its mock-epic sea voyage preludes with nymphomaniacal sirens and men using their erect penises for masts, and the narrative takes off when a gust of wind lifts the ship to the Moon. Back on Earth, the crew witnesses a battle among giants who sail about "on vast islands the way we do on our war galleys."

Before *Utopia*, More's most significant publications were translations of Lucian, on which he collaborated with Erasmus. Lucian was said to have spoken the truth through laughter; Erasmus later told a correspondent to read *Utopia* "if you want a laugh." *Utopia* drew on Plato for logistics and on Lucian for outrageousness of storytelling.

The archetypal island paradise became fixed in *Utopia*—you need a fool of a sea captain to get there—but it wasn't long before it started moving again. After More, utopias explored advances in naval technology. The conception of the perfect world itself began to change and shift.

While Francis Bacon's *New Atlantis* (1617) looks to the distant past, when the science of navigation "was greater than at this day" (think Noah), Tommaso Campanella's *The City of the Sun*

(1623) looks to the future, when vessels would move not with oars or wind but "by a marvelous contrivance." After James Watt proved Campanella right, it was utopian authors who anticipated ships would become as much home as vehicle. Etienne Cabet's *Travels in Icaria* (1839) describes a ferry that offers drawing rooms with fireplaces and cabins outfitted with "all the . . . furnishings one might need," and Theodor Herzl's Jewish utopia, *Old-New Land* (1902), depicts the repopulation of the Promised Land via a vessel called *Futuro** that features an onboard orchestra and a daily newspaper. One delighted passenger never leaves, declaring, "This ship is Zion!"

In 1833, J. A. Etzler, a German inventor, proposed a fleet of huge propeller-powered landmasses closer to *True History*'s "war galleys" than Cabet's or Herzl's protoluxury liners. Etzler un-got the joke of Lucian. *The Paradise Within the Reach of All Men, Without Labor, by Powers of Nature and Machinery*, describes floating islands large enough for gardens and palaces, with room for "thousands of families," and promises inhabitants the ability to "roam over the whole world . . . in all security, refinements of social life, comforts and luxury." The islands could be built in a decade, he said, if only he found enough investors. He never did.

Six decades later Jules Verne returned the idea to fiction with *The Floating Island* (1895), a novel as cautionary as it is utopian. The book begins a stone's throw from Utopia Road. The carriage of a French chamber quartet breaks down twenty miles north of San Diego. The hapless musicians wander

---

* The *Futuro* is surely of the same class as the *Fantasy*, the vessel that carried Johann Andreae's religious pilgrim to *Christianopolis* (1619).

onto a massive, docked "Floating Island" filled with millionaires, nouveau riche robber barons who have shoved off to a
different kind of life. The vessel is a perfect oval of five thousand acres, driven by hundreds of propellers and two dynamos
that produce ten million horsepower. Floating Island's main
town is Milliard City. The population is ten thousand, its army
five hundred strong. The chamber group is contracted to offer
performances for the mobile civilization, and for a time they
are delighted. Yvernès, the first violin, anticipates that "the
twentieth century would not end before the seas were ploughed
by floating towns."

Floating Island encounters various dangers—pirates, volcanoes, wild animals. Halfway through the book, the Floating Island Company Ltd. appoints a liquidator. "The Company had
gone under," pun intended. The millionaires produce the obvious solution—they buy the vessel themselves. $400 million later
they're back to island hopping. But Verne will not permit utopia
to last. In a clumsy deus ex machina, the unsinkable Floating
Island begins to break apart, embodying tensions brewing between characters for hundreds of pages. The island snaps and
sinks.

A century later, in 2002, French architect Jean-Philippe Zoppini un-got the joke of Verne. He proposed several designs based
on *The Floating Island*. The shipyard that built the *Queen Mary
II* agreed to construct Zoppini's vessal if anyone came along
with the funds and infrastructure to operate it. None did.

58

On my second day in Norway, in the living room of his Oslo home, Kloster and I embarked again on discussions of the discussions of his story that we might eventually have.

The home reminded me of a Russian dacha: wide open spaces, furniture from a range of centuries and cultures, original art on the walls that intimidated by looking a little familiar. Kloster was doubting himself again, and I found myself offering a pep talk to an earnest, broken utopian.

I'd found a book that included a reference to a certain Knud Rasmussen Kloster from 1825, a man "of an old seafaring family," but the Kloster shipping empire hadn't truly begun its rise until the twentieth century. It started with ice. Kloster's grandfather hauled blocks by the shipload from northern Norway before refrigeration, and his father moved the business into oil when deposits were discovered in the North Sea. For a time the Kloster tanker fleet was as large as any in the world. Kloster studied naval architecture at M.I.T., and took over the family business at thirty. He set the company on a new tack almost at once, constructing a nine-thousand-ton ship called the *Sunward* to ferry British retirees to Gibraltar. Kloster's visionary streak poked through even then: The *Sunward* offered amenities unusual for a ferry—overnight cabins, onboard restaurants.

The Gibraltar plan snagged when Franco claimed the peninsula in a final power grab. As Britain and Spain waged a miniature cold war, Kloster was left with a ship but nowhere to sail it.

In Florida, future Carnival Cruise Line founder Ted Arison had precisely the opposite problem. He had built an infrastructure to fill a hole in the Caribbean cruise industry, but the Israeli vessel he had leased was recalled as a troop transport for the Six-Day War of 1967. He had a destination but no ship.

Arison rang up Kloster, and three weeks later the *Sunward* arrived in Miami.

The partnership was wildly successful—they added the *Starward*, the *Skyward*, and the *Southward*—but Norwegian Cruise Lines (NCL) wound up in court. Kloster and Arison were different kinds of capitalists. Arison was ruthless. Kloster wound up in tears on the deck of the *Sunward* reading Charles Reich's *The Greening of America*. Kloster held to capitalism like a faith but tempered it with conscience and a belief that the cruise industry was uniquely positioned to battle back against cultural alienation and malaise—to become a medium for global communication.

The lawsuit ended with Arison retreating for the time being and Kloster moving to Florida to take over. In 1972, he envisioned a wholly new kind of ship. In an address titled "The Shape of Things to Come," delivered to British travel agents in Vienna, Kloster quoted Emerson and laid out plans for a split-hull catamaran-style "ultra-modern design" that would offer both an onboard observatory for astronomy and an underwater observation room for the study of marine life. The ship was no longer just a ship. Vessels of the future, Kloster told the agents, must serve as a "nexus" for three groups of people: those who visit them, those who live and work on them, and those who are visited by them.

In 1979, NCL was ready to move beyond words. The company bought the world's last great ocean liner, the *France*, overhauling and rechristening it. The *Norway* was a paradigm shift. To that point it was believed that twenty thousand tons was about as large as a cruise ship could get and still count on a profit. The *Norway* tripled that overnight—and profited just fine. The ship featured a variety of shops and boutiques along "streets" called Champs-Elysées and Fifth Avenue.

Kloster hailed the "megaship" as "a destination in and of itself."

Thirty years later, Kloster was the nice guy who had finished last. Arison had rebounded, using money that was rightfully Kloster's to start what would eventually become the largest cruise company in the world. In the eighties, Kloster bet everything he had on the Phoenix Project—and lost.

59

In his living room, as I tried to convince him his story was worth telling, Kloster stared me down with a look that combined disbelief and corporate savvy.

He had an idea. He produced a small model of the underside of a boat, a tandem rudder system, and placed it on the coffee table between us.

"Say you are in a large ship. It is moving toward an island, some rocks. You need to turn—turn quickly."

He explained that when ships reach a certain tonnage, single-rudder systems snap from the pressure exerted on them. The solution was a second, much smaller rudder positioned behind the first. This rudder was called a "trim tab." The trim tab rudder turned the *wrong way*, shifting the current and creating a vacuum so that the larger rudder could turn the right way without breaking. Kloster demonstrated this with the model between his knees, moving the rudders back and forth and steering his hypothetical ship away from the rocks. The trim tab rudder lent itself to metaphor—engineer Buckminster Fuller had been the first to suggest that it demonstrated "what one little man could do"—but sitting across from Kloster I was baffled.

He stared at me. I asked for the toilet.

When I came out Kloster acted defeated and offhandedly showed me his home office. It was modest, a square meter beside the washroom—the office not of a mariner, but a submariner. The walls were jammed with bound collections of the correspondence that Kloster had conducted while attempting to bring the Phoenix Project to pass. The room was a dead child's shrine—Kloster didn't want to talk about it, but he wouldn't throw it all away, either. Now I understood. Kloster was the trim tab. He had turned himself the wrong way to steer us all clear of the rocks.* It was the dilemma of all earnest utopians.

"If there's nothing here, then why are you keeping all these?"

"That's a good question." He shrugged. "There *is* a story here. Someday someone may want to know about it."

---

* Looking back on the nineteenth century, the narrator of *Looking Backward* describes his troubled society as "dragging anchor and in danger of going adrift. Whither it would drift nobody could say, but all feared the rocks."

60

The World was the creation of Kloster's son, another Knut Kloster Jr. Kloster had two sons, and both had had ideas for innovative cruise ships. One was *The World*, the other, if it ever came to pass, a floating beach resort. Like the father of prodigal twins, Kloster denied that either plan had anything at all to do with his Phoenix Project.

The World, however, fit neatly into the history. After its first sail, the ship struck the same reef as Verne's Floating Island. Its management company lost $100 million struggling through the climate of the post-9/11 travel industry. Their lender foreclosed, tried to run the ship on its own, and lost another $150 million. The future looked bleak until the residents stumbled onto the same solution as Verne's millionaires: They bought it.

"The ship is now a co-op," said the *San Francisco Chronicle*.

61

I stepped onboard *The World* just in time to attend a crew recognition ceremony in the Colosseo, the ship's theater. Almost the entire staff had gathered so that Captain Ola Harsheim, a man who looked exactly like what you'll imagine if I tell you to imagine a self-portrait of van Gogh, could offer congratulations to various crewmen on their years of service. The crew's lodgings on the lower decks of the ship—the decks without verandas—made it easy to liken *The World* to a floating version of Fourier's retch-inducing phalansteries. Before Brook Farm, Fourier's vision had remained largely bourgeois, and his

perfect society retained class distinctions. Nevertheless, a be-
nign expression of "community" was on the lips of both residents and staff of *The World* for my entire stay. We're all in
the same boat, they said.

After the ceremony I was shown to my room. Mine was one of
several spaces onboard that had been compiled out of two studio
apartments during a period of reorganization, and as my rooms
were mirror images of each other the apartment had an odd dou-
bling quality to it. I had two bathrooms, and two verandas with
two sliding glass doors. I had two flat-screen televisions, but only
one kitchen, only one bottle of champagne waiting for me, and
only one bathtub (double-size). A number of strategically placed
mirrors expanded space and provided another source of dou-
bling—or quadrupling—the result being that at one moment I
could look through the pocket doors into one room and not be
entirely certain that I was not already standing there, and at another glance into a chamber and experience a kind of vampire
thrill at not seeing a reflection where I expected one. The apartment was a homey fun house, which was another way of saying
that I sometimes got lost in it. It was one of the smallest spaces
onboard.

I stepped out onto one of my verandas just as some Swede,
down by the dock, took a picture of the ship with me in it. In
some ports, *The World* is a spectacle.

Lewis Mumford: "The autonomous machine, in its dual
capacity as a universal instrument and invisible object of collective worship, itself has become utopia."

It took another French architect and the U.S. military to make the Phoenix Project even conceivable.

"If we forget for a moment that a steamship is a machine for transport and look at it with a fresh eye," wrote Le Corbusier in 1931, "we shall feel that we are facing an important manifestation of temerity, of discipline, of harmony, of a beauty that is calm, vital, and strong." The son of a watchmaker, Le Corbusier was fond of saying a house was a machine to live in. In *Towards a New Architecture,* he argued that ocean liners already rivaled the world's most impressive structures.

Le Corbusier went on to design buildings that looked like ships and proposed apartment living with maid service, a kitchen staff, and a communal dining room like a luxury vessel. He insisted that "the steamship is the first stage in the realization of a world organized according to the new spirit."

At about the same time the U.S. military was getting serious about bringing back the old floating island idea. Edward R. Armstrong—once a circus strongman, later an engineer and inventor—proposed a battery of "seadromes," floating airports that would enable fighter planes to hopscotch the Atlantic. The plan caught FDR's eye, but advances in aircraft flight ranges made them obsolete. Another war-era plan was the top-secret Project Habakkuk, named for a biblical prophet ("Thou didst tread the sea with thy horses": Habakkuk 3:15) and reportedly a favorite of Churchill's. It was an artificial iceberg: a huge vessel made of "pykrete," an ice and sawdust blend that rendered it impervious to torpedo strikes.

Habakkuk never came to pass either. But the floating island concept would never fade from the military imagination. After the seadrome the basic concept underwent periodic revision: the "megafloat" and the "mobile offshore base." In 1996, plans were drawn for the "Joint Mobile Offshore Base," a multimodule platform like a floating Guantánamo, featuring an artificial beach for hovercraft, space for a POW camp, and room for 3,500 vehicles, 150 aircraft, and 3,000 troops. It was Lucian's war galley with airports and Quonset huts, one of the "Floating Fortresses" that patrol the Atlantic in Orwell's *1984*.

I was given a tour of the public areas of *The World*, what in ship parlance was called "the Village." The main hallway through the Village was "the Street," and along it were the theater, a small sanctuary space, a (very) high-end jewelry store, an equally impressive boutique, a deli for gourmet foods or simple groceries, a cigar lounge, a small casino, an Internet café, a four-thousand-volume library, a handful of restaurants, a couple bars, and a spa that sported quasispiritual massage facilities and a state-of-the-art gym. *The World* had been criticized as something of a ghost ship, and it was true that a lot of the time it didn't seem like there were many folks around: The shops and the casino never opened while I was onboard. But the residents argued that if others wanted a lot of cruise zaniness, late-night parties and lines for dinner, they were welcome to it. It was not for them. Their apartments were not staterooms where they slept while on vacation. They were homes.

I was shown what a couple of the larger homes looked like. The first was a bigger, grander version of my own apartment, a space that was for rent while the owner was not onboard. It went for some thousands per night. The second would have suited Captain Nemo. Each of the three bedrooms had its own bathroom, the whole place was paneled, and the veranda that wrapped around a corner of the ship was an extra room furnished as exquisitely as the interior. I remember round windows, a ship's wheel, a giant square-rigger in a bottle (that might be imagination), and the master bedroom had its own veranda and what my guide called "a religious experience of a closet." This was more typical. The residents spent a good deal of time customizing their spaces, and the upper-tier staff said they'd been surprised at how unique the apartments could be made to look, transformed and modified, sometimes with furnishings, sometimes with art worth more than the apartment itself.

I met no one who had seen every space onboard.

I had dinner that night with James St. John, the CEO of ResidenSea, the resident-owned company that managed *The World*. We ate at East, the ship's Asian restaurant. The ship actually had too many restaurants—they opened on a rotating schedule—but East was a favorite. All of the restaurants offered outdoor eating when weather permitted; the annual victual budget was $4 million. Later, I stopped by the Colosseo to see a local group (sax, bongos, harp, accordion, xylophone) rush through a variety of show tunes so they could disembark before the ship left Sweden. After the show I met an older couple walking through the Village. They liked the performance, they said, but they were fonder of the ship's lecture series. Wherever *The World* went, it was accompanied by a team of scholar–tour guides who gave talks that put the region into historical context. The ship was now in the middle of its "Bothnian Expedition."

"You kind of schedule your day around it," the woman said.

It was their second time onboard; they were thinking of buying an apartment. They were renters, but came for stays of six to eight weeks. I converted weeks to dollars.

"That's a good chunk of—time."

"It is," the man said. "And now it's time to go to sleep."

I wandered the Village. The cigar lounge was empty; the chess tables in the game room had no pieces. *The World* was less like a ghost ship, I thought, than an amusement park you'd leased. Or bought. At an empty bar on deck 11, I chatted with a Filipino barman. He knew my name somehow. He'd been on the ship since the beginning and had traveled around the world several times as a result. An hour after the engines grumbled to life, he looked out the window and became excited.

"Mr. Hallman—we're moving!"

We stepped out to the rail to watch the land slink by, passing steel foundries on the edge of Luleå, their towers topped by a blue and spectral fire, the negative signature of heat. Below us the Gulf of Bothnia was a dark winter's sea, choppy and pleated in moonlight, like skin viewed through a microscope.

"This may be the last time I see Sweden," I allowed.

"Really." There was a touch of pity in the barman's voice.

64

It was Fuller—of trim tab fame—who was the first to marry Le Corbusier's maritime idealism with something that actually had a chance to hit the water. Early in the 1960s, a Japanese patron commissioned Fuller to create a "tetrahedronal floating city" for Tokyo Bay. Fuller designed three floating cities: one for harbors, one for semiprotected waters; and one for deep sea. In *Utopia or Oblivion*, Fuller cited a claim that visions for perfect worlds failed because they were unrealistic from the get-go. Ship design, however, offered hope, as it required a different sort of design discipline. All of a ship's functions had to be understood comprehensively in advance. If you were unrealistic, you sank.

Fuller's patron died in 1966, which cleared the way for the U.S. Department of Housing and Urban Development to get interested. HUD passed the tetrahedronal city on to the navy, which deemed it both water-worthy and economically feasible. Baltimore, Maryland, remained interested in a city for the Chesapeake Bay until LBJ, also a fan of the plan, left office. Johnson took two of Fuller's models to his presidential library in Texas. They're still there.

After Fuller's Japanese patron died, the cruise business was born anew of the unholy matrimony of Kloster and Arison, and for the next decade and a half Kloster charted the industry's course with a kind of moral sextant. NCL bought an island and a few of its rivals. In 1984, the *Norway* was the largest cruise ship in the world, and the company dominated the business.

Then Kloster suggested an even wilder revolution.

Others had followed NCL's lead in converting old ocean liners, but now there were none left. The only option for a revolutionary ship was to build one from scratch. Describing the initial planning of the Phoenix Project, Kloster said, "The design objective was to give passengers a sense of community. . . . We talked about a 'downtown' featuring broad streets and village squares, lined with shops, boutiques and restaurants, nightclubs, cinemas. . . . In short, a city afloat."

The *Phoenix* would exceed 250,000 gross tons, quadruple the size of the *Norway*. Its aft split-hull would serve as a marina for four day cruisers, each with the passenger capacity of the *Sunward*. Kloster announced "the dawn of a new age at sea," and the plan came to include a number of smaller ships that, acting as remora to the *Phoenix*, would amount to a "global Chautauqua circuit."

65

The strange symbol on my document wallet—the symbol of *The World*—was not a picture of a ship. It was an island.

The original frontispiece of *Utopia* was a visual joke featuring not just one island, but two. It's generally held that the shape of Utopia—a nearly circular crescent whose points almost touch, making for a large inner harbor—comes from Plato's description of Atlantis.

Plato, it's been suggested, may have been thinking of the Greek island of Santorini, which is crescent-shaped and has smaller islands situated between its points. This suggested to Plato a tactically perfect location to erect a fortress that would make one's inner harbor impenetrable. Atlantis and Utopia each have such an island and fortress.

A critical difference: Utopia did not start out as an island. It was a peninsula when the land was first conquered by King Utopus. Utopus dredges the nar-

row band of earth connecting it to the mainland, snipping its figurative umbilicus and delivering the infant of a better world. That Utopia was now suspiciously womb-shaped nodded both to Hesiod's Elysium, whose island paradise was swaddled in the ocean's amniotic fluid, and to Simon Magus, whose Eden was comfortably in utero. More hyperextended the metaphor. An inner harbor guarded by a jutting phallic tower, and a perspective shift from three dimensions to two, made the book jacket of *Utopia* a rather clinical depiction of coitus.

Erasmus once suggested that the only thing that kept More from a monk's life was his sexual appetite.

I would sail with *The World* from Luleå to Vaasa, Finland, and then down the Finnish coast to Mariehamn in the Åland Islands, a curious archipelago in the mouth of the Gulf. The islands technically belonged to Finland, but the population spoke Swedish, and they were recognized by the United Nations as autonomous. The tactically advantageous location of

the Ålands had long been known, though it wasn't until centuries after More that anyone tried to build a fortress there—first the Swedes, then the Russians. Nevertheless, it seemed perfectly reasonable to wonder whether More, in designing Utopia in Antwerp (far closer to Finland than Greece), might not have been thinking of Bothnia rather than Plato.

We were sailing through the protected inner harbor of Utopia.

66

I woke at 5:00 A.M. to a peach-colored world, the chill blue water stripping by at seventeen knots, a warm wind puffing my curtains, and a sound like light surf rising from the waterline. From the bathtub's window I watched the first spark of sun ignite the horizon, and room service brought a light breakfast. The ship had encountered gale-force winds and four-meter waves overnight, but the captain had deployed the stabilizers, the ship's ten-meter wings, and we barely felt the heavy seas. Coffee woke me a little, but from that point in my voyage on, as though the secret sharer of my subconscious recognized the feel of warm, moist containment and the possibility of months-long rest, I would be torn between trying to see the ship and just coming back to my apartment, my home, to survey the Gulf and to sleep. It was—think of More's puns, please—a womb with a view.

After breakfast I went back to sleep on the spot where sunlight had warmed the bed.

The ship had arranged a Thai lemongrass oil massage for late morning, and my masseuse apologized for the lack of candles and incense (ship regulations) before she went to work ("Mr. Hallman, put your face in the hole, please, sir"). I met St. John for lunch and then a tour of the back of the house. He was a jolly chap, something like the Skipper from *Gilligan's Island*, another fool of a sea captain. St. John had once considered the seminary, but life had tacked, and time in the military, in the hotel business, in the shipping business, and finally as the manager of a private community on Jupiter Island, Florida, left him with the perfect résumé for *The World*.

As we climbed downstairs, St. John insisted that *The World* was the cleanest ship in the industry. As above, the main hallway in the back of the house was a "street." It was utilitarian, but tidy. There were two below-deck saloons, an officers' club and a crew bar, but in keeping with the lean-toward-egalitarian theme of the ship, staff, officers, and crew mixed freely. We visited the mooring decks as a team of men were tying us off to the dock in Vaasa with cleats the size of anvils and capstans the size of barrels. We visited the recycling facility. Ecological progressiveness was one of the few traits common among the residents, St. John said, and the ship, in addition to being the first vessel of its class to run on industrial diesel instead of heavy bunker fuel, took pains to recover as much of its waste as it could. Everything not crushed and stored for recycling was incinerated—including sewage.

"We even capture our ash," St. John said.

The residents' routine was morning exercise in the pools, or a walk on the track or on treadmills in the gym, and a leisurely breakfast as the ship pulled into port. Some vacated their apartments early so that the crew could get their work out of the way and go ashore for the day. The residents did the same, either renting cars for private excursions or signing up for prearranged tours that were announced in several onboard publications and on the ship's morning TV news show. I didn't disembark for a day or two. I played Pebble Beach on the ship's high-tech golf simulator, I lunched with the captain, and I got a peek at the cargo van–sized engines and the onboard water-treatment facility that could produce three times the two hundred tons of fresh water the ship used daily.

I went to a lecture about the Åland Islands. The archipelago sat right on an ancient line between hunter-gatherer and agrarian civilization, and the lecturer offered us his theory on how the Ålands' aborigines, who butchered people and seals alike and buried them all in the same mound graveyards, eventually became cultural Swedes but Fin nationals. The Gulf of Bothnia was curious not just for the Ålands, he said, but for the fact that it was all becoming slowly shallower.

The islands were moving—up.

67

The *Phoenix* pitted Kloster against his family. The strain began when NCL took off; the *Phoenix* was simply too risky. Kloster stepped down from the chairmanship in 1986, divesting himself entirely, taking only the plan with him. He turned his full attention to bringing the *Phoenix* to pass. A team formed around the effort and came to include administrators of maritime organizations, two former admirals, and a former commandant of the Coast Guard. Various retrofits of the blueprint saw the ship renamed *Phoenix World City* and *America World City.* When it turned out that the vision future-shocked everyone it touched, the America World City marketing team turned to the imagery of Le Corbusier to sell it.

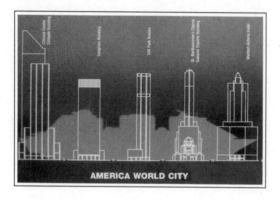

It didn't work. *America World City* came closest to being built in 1989, but Citicorp pulled out at the meeting that would close the deal. Kloster suspected Arison was involved. In 1996, Westin Resorts and Hotels backed the project, but the ship's in-house champion was ousted in a squabble over personalities. It stalled there.

At about the same time, Kloster's son's vision was just hitting the drawing board. *The World* suffered through five years of downsizing before construction began.

"This is the new lifestyle," the younger Kloster said when *The World* finally got wet. "To travel the world without leaving home."

68

On my last day onboard I was invited along with forty or so residents to visit a few sites of interest in the Ålands. We assembled in the Village, filed down the gangway, piled onto a chartered bus. The residents were millionaires to a man, but as we pulled away they chattered and laughed like kids riding home from school.

"They're affluent people, but warm," I'd been told, the caveat added as though it ran contrary to expectation.

Which made me wonder whether *The World*, beyond allowing you to stay at home while you traveled, offered the possibility of community, of kinship, to those whose success tended to alienate them. It may be wasted compassion to empathize with the wealthy, but it seemed to me that the wealthy remained apart not because they liked being apart but because an economic system that encouraged class division—a system in which not everyone was in the same boat—chopped people into insoluble bits: wealthy and poor, cold and warm. Dichotomies. Did utopia have to eliminate class? Could a class system figure out how to retain dignity for all involved—without inducing vomiting? Was Fourier right? Was that the best possible world? *The World* was born of capitalism, but it seemed to me that it took at least one step toward transcending it. It wasn't just the community onboard—the resident poker game that sprouted up spontaneously or the karaoke nights that revealed the wealthy had the same plebian tastes as everyone else. It was, too, a conspicuous lack of currency, of transactions, onboard; it was the green values they embraced not because it was profitable but because they thought it right; it was the government they had formed themselves, intentionally, when they bought the ship.

"By the way," St. John told me, "I don't think it's utopia." I wasn't so sure.

Among the sights we were on our way to see in Mariehamn were the fortresses that had tried to take tactical advantage of the Ålands that More and Plato prescribed. The Swedish castle stood boxy and tall but had failed to fend off the Russians, who made it only halfway into their own fort before ten thousand Frenchmen and forty British ships under Nelson brought it to the ground. It was another of *The World*'s lecturers—Noel Broadbent, an anthropologist with the Smithsonian—who told us this story as we stood before the ruins of one of the fortress's walls. The residents wandered, petting the cold, thick cannon still in place and admiring the impact marks of British ball.

We went home to the ship.

I left the following morning, taking the same plane out of Mariehamn as Broadbent. We chatted in the tiny airport. I likened *The World* to a votive ship we had seen in a church on our tour the day before. Common in Scandinavia, the model ships hanging from church ceilings symbolized the spiritual journey of the early Christian community. Broadbent nodded, but thought *The World* was closer to something from the work of Swedish poet Harry Martinson, who had mulled real-life merchant marine experiences in books of poems called *Ghost Ship* and *Trade Winds*. Then Martinson shared the 1974 Nobel

Prize in Literature for an epic poem called *Aniara: A Review of Man in Time and Space*, which imagined huge space vessels called Goldondas ferrying émigrés from a polluted Earth to a better Mars.

"It's an interesting concept," Broadbent said, when we'd taken our seats in the island-hopper to Stockholm. "If you're self-contained—if you can do it on your own—then you're almost like those sci-fi stories of ships carrying civilization off after cataclysm. It's not far from that. And islands are not so different. They're moving, too—in geologic time. Either way, it's all about boundaries and travel."

As the plane banked up, we had a view of *The World* at its mooring, as large as the city beside it but small as a toy from our vantage.

69

"I was depressed all yesterday," Kloster told me on my last day in Norway.

I wasn't supposed to see him at all—his German shepherd had fallen ill and needed to go to the vet—but then the plan changed. When we met in the lobby Kloster was sad not because of the dog, but again because he thought his story was uninteresting.

We drove down to Oslo's fjord. Several cruise ships were docked monolithically alongside the city. Kloster's walruslike benevolence gave him the naïve serenity of a mystic. He pretended not to notice a prostitute streetwalking the pier.

We visited a series of maritime museums together. The first was dedicated to Thor Heyerdahl's *Kon-Tiki* expedition.

If Heyerdahl's ocean crossing on a balsa-wood raft dabbled usefully with the past, I thought, then Kloster's imaginary megaship had tinkered with the future. The second was devoted to unearthed Viking ships. I climbed a parapet to look down into the ancient wooden hulls, then glanced back at Kloster in the middle of a hallway, tourists streaming around him as though he were an atoll. The last museum was a tribute to Norway's shipping business, a gallery of models and to-scale mock-ups of tiny crew quarters. We walked directly to the back of the museum and found the original miniature of the *Sunward*, set without fanfare among notable old tankers.

After Kloster left NCL, the company abandoned his guiding principles, his "process of vision." It sailed into a whirlpool of bad luck and bad publicity. They reflagged their vessels in the Bahamas, dumped labor agreements that protected Third World staff, and tried to go public in 1987, only to have their initial public offering fall on the day after Black Monday. In the nineties they tried to reverse course with a more aggressive approach but were already taking on water. Eventually even Arison joined in the bidding when the company was put on the auction block.

After the final deal to realize *America World City* petered out, Kloster became a different kind of utopian, proposing smaller projects that were even greater long shots. In 2001, he suggested a seventy-story glass globe for the World Trade Center memorial called "Planet Earth at Ground Zero." A year later he wrote to then secretary-general of the United Nations Kofi Annan proposing *Gaiaship*, a goodwill vessel that could be paid for, he suggested, if all the countries of the world contributed one tenth of 1 percent of their military budgets.

Arthur C. Clarke wrote a letter of support—he called ocean liners a "microcosm of the Earth"—but an aide to Annan rejected the proposal.

In the meantime, Kloster's original vision kept creeping toward reality.

After the *Norway*, cruise ships started getting bigger. In the eighties, a number of ships came in at around 40,000 tons, and in 1988 the *Sovereign of the Seas* upped the ante to 73,000 tons. Carnival Cruise Line broke 100,000 tons in 1996, only to be eclipsed two years later by the *Grand Princess* at 109,000 tons. More followed—142,000, 151,000, 160,000. Recently, Royal Caribbean launched the Genesis Project, a 225,000-ton vessel with seven "neighborhoods," twenty-one pools, and twenty-four restaurants. Similarly, *The World* can spot competitors in dry dock: Residential Cruise Line plans a luxury ship called *Magellan*; Condo Cruise Lines International claims 90 percent sales on a plan to convert old cruise ships to condominiums; and Utopia Residences Co. has promised a $1.1 billion, 105,000-ton ship called *Utopia* with two hundred cabins and a "Philanthropy Office" to track residents' good deeds.

"The luxury of new views every day," said the *St. Louis Post-Dispatch*.

At the shipping museum, Kloster and I came around to the model of the *Norway*. It had its own glass case—a ship in a bottle. Kloster showed me how the *Norway* differed from newer monstrosities: It was small enough that its hull was curved all the way around. More recent ships were boxier, their cross sections interchangeable. Each section of the *Norway* was unique.

"It was a good ship," Kloster said, as though speaking over the remains of a man in state, one who had lived long and perhaps made a difference. Kloster went a bit woozy looking through the glass. The *Norway* had had a tough run. In 2001, it sprouted dozens of leaks in its sprinkler system, earning fines, and two years later an explosion in its boiler room killed eight. It was decommissioned not long after.

I asked Kloster where it was now. He said he'd heard it was lying on a beach in India, but he wasn't sure.

"It's okay." His lips found a smile for the first time all day. "A ship can't last forever."

A MEAL

People await the end of the world, or a cosmic renewal, or the Golden Age, especially in times of profound crisis; they herald the imminence of an earthly paradise to defend themselves against the despair provoked by extreme misery, the loss of liberty, and the collapse of all traditional values.

—MIRCEA ELIADE,
History of Religious Ideas

In the context of pragmatic social science, utopian thinking at once falls into place. Utopian ideas may be practical hypotheses, that is, expedients for pilot experimentation. Or they may be stimuli for response, so that people get to know what they themselves mean.

—PAUL GOODMAN,
Utopian Essays and Practical Proposals

70

In the early 1960s, self-actualization theorist Abraham Maslow, perhaps frustrated that spatial utopias—mobile or no—had stalled trying to create perfect worlds and perfect people, set out to approach the question somewhat differently. "There is no Garden of Eden," he wrote, "there is no paradise, there is no heaven except for a passing moment or two." Which did not mean one should give up trying to make a better world. Rather, Maslow said, one should settle for exactly that: better. He imagined an isolated island civilization populated by one thousand self-actualized people. How good would a self-actualized society become? He didn't know—it depended on how good people could become given the limitations of human nature. The important part was to note that the utopian spirit was really an attempt at psychological improvement. In other words, utopia wasn't a place at all. "We might, if we wished, call this simply 'planning.'" The perfect world became a better state of mind. Maslow called his better psychological state "Eupsychia."

Eupsychian Management (1965) spells out the necessary preconditions for a eupsychian society: Self-actualized persons are motivated, healthy, just, and, above all, improvable. To demonstrate this last point, Maslow cited a 1935 study of nutrition and chicken behavior.* The study had discovered that some chickens were good "choosers" of food, while others were poor. In a "cafeteria" situation, the good-choosing chickens opted for a healthy combination of corn meal, wheat bran, and oyster-shell flour, resulting in better feathers, better sex drive, better growth rates, and additional better food. "The superior [chickens] choose foods which supply the nutrients for that superiority and in so doing are wise," the study asserted. The poor-choosing chickens suffered predictably. From there, the study tested a theory: What if you gave the good-choosers' diet to the poor-choosing chickens? It worked: The poor-choosers never became quite as strong and healthy as the good-choosers, but the evidence was clear—chickens were improvable.

As people should be, Maslow concluded. He never explored it himself, but the further implication was that a better state of mind, a eupsychia, could be brought about with better food.

71

Which, actually, was an idea that had been bouncing around in utopian literature—either in jest or in earnest—for about as long as it had existed.

In utopian literature food mirrors mores. How an imaginary society prepares and takes a meal betrays its values as communal and social or sensual and indulgent. In Plato and Aristotle, the consumption of food is left to the equivalent of chow halls.

* "A Study of Individuality in the Nutritive Instincts and of the Causes and Effects of Variations in the Selection of Food," W. Franklin Dove, *American Naturalist*, vol. 69, no. 724 (1935), pp. 469–544.

By way of contrast, Athenaeus, a Greek-Egyptian grammarian from the third century, redacted thousand-year-old stories of a glutton's paradise to a fifteen-volume account of a single luxurious supper. Scholars, however, claim *The Banquet of the Learned* distorted the "bantering spirit" of its sources.

Athenaeus didn't get the joke.

A bantering spirit was surely behind a variety of well-fed utopias that sustained the alimentary imagination through the Middle Ages. *The Decameron* records a mythical Basque paradise called Bengodi that features a mountain of grated Parmesan cheese and a river of white wine, and the Land of Cockaigne, a food Eden described in countless poems across Europe ("Thogh Paradis be miri and bright / Cockaigne is of fairer sight"), is similarly equipped with creeks of oil, honey, and milk. To my eye, Pieter Brueghel the Elder's 1567 painting "The Land of

Cockaigne" suggests there was more than "met and drink" being consumed in paradise, and a general theme of wild indulgence would be even more fully embraced in Rabelais's naughty monastery, the Abbey of Thélème.

Both Brueghel and Rabelais followed More, and Rabelais at least knew *Utopia*: Epistolary bits of *Gargantua* list Utopia as a return address. More's Utopians had taken a step toward the indulgent life—but just a step. They begin meals with bits of improvisational literature and attend them with scents and music, but dispense with supper quickly "so that nobody gets bored."

72

After the Renaissance, the bantering spirit all but disappeared.

Utopian novels often have a predictable premise to go along with the predictable romantic subplot: A protagonist adventurer stumbles onto paradise, generally via cataclysm—e.g., shipwreck—and is forthwith introduced to a knowledgeable companion who acts as docent on a guided tour of a variety of social advances. Nearly all utopias leave room for a discussion of food. Louis Sebastien Mercier's *Memoirs of the Year* 2500 (1771), for example, claims that its society has successfully "balanced the interest of the grocer and the consumer." William Morris's design utopia, *News from Nowhere* (1890), describes a dinner in which a cook's love of craft is apparent, but there is "no excess either of quantity or of gourmandize." And long after Aldous Huxley spent his dystopian angst in *Brave New World*, he concocted *Island* (1961), a spiritual utopia that nibbles bits from yoga, tantric sex therapy, and Scientology and prescribes a kind of prayer-chewing during meals that owes its inspiration to nineteenth-century chew guru Horace Fletcher.

At just about the same time the whole world was "Fletcherizing," an important shift was taking place in how visionaries attempted to implement their visions of perfection. As early as the English civil war, the utopian novel had begun a transformation into ideological pamphlet and constitution-writing, a shift that set the utopian spirit on the path to absolute perfection that Maslow would later lament. It wasn't until the nineteenth century that utopian plans threatened to realize outside fiction. Marx and Engels, borrowing heavily from Owen, Fourier, and Saint-Simon, led the charge. Engels's *Socialism: From Utopia to Science* (1880) marks a fair date for, and describes the basic thinking behind, the transition from small-scale social experimentation to the philosophical treatise aimed at revolution. Utopian blueprint became political manifesto.

Of the many movements that would come to proclaim themselves with manifestos, at least two—both Italian—made food a central feature of their revolutionary paradigm. One was a joke; the other dead serious.

73

Lettres de Malaisie (1897) by French writer Paul Adam is a curious addition to the utopian genre in that its ideal society is founded by fictional followers of actual utopian reformers—Proudhon, Cabet, Fourier. In other words, it's a utopian novel about a utopia inspired by utopian experimentation itself inspired by earlier utopian novels. *Lettres de Malaisie* deviates from classic tropes only in that its male protagonist is attended by two docents instead of one (both, as it happens, charming women), who provide him with the typical sampler plate of improved schools, courts of law, religious institutions, army, technology, sexual practices, and, of course, food. But it wasn't Adam who would be first to aim for a food eupsychia. The most important contribution of *Lettres de Malaísie* may be that it caught the attention of Italian nationalist and future Futurist aeropoet F. T. Marinetti.

Marinetti was interested in food long before he set out to change—and, according to Ezra Pound, succeeded in changing—the way the whole world thought about art. After an Egyptian youth and an aborted attempt to follow his father into law, Marinetti set off on a peculiar literary career. Sarah Bernhardt presented one of his poems at her salon; he published a volume ominously titled *Destruction*; and a play, *Le Roi Bombance*, caused a small riot when it opened.

Le Roi Bombance was dedicated to Paul Adam.

The plot reveals Marinetti was thinking food: The royal cook of the "cockaignesque" kingdom of Bourdes has died; his assistants feign preparations for a banquet to quell the political crisis that ensues; the local population revolts when they realize they've been tricked; the king and the remaining cooks are all consumed in a gustatory orgy; and finally a character called Saint Putrefaction, accompanied by a vampire called Ptiokaroum, resuscitates the consumed characters in a hard-to-stage but surely thrilling emesis-cum-resurrection.

Critics acknowledge that *Le Roi Bombance* isn't much of a play. But why was a dramatically dystopian vision—of any quality—dedicated to the author of a utopian novel? It wasn't the only time Marinetti was influenced by Adam. In 1905, Marinetti wrote "To the Automobile," a poem launching the celebration of speed that would be central to the Futurist movement. It drew on the description of a road trip from an earlier Adam novel.

"To the Automobile" proved as much omen as ode. Marinetti's father died in 1907, leaving a significant inheritance. Marinetti bought a Fiat and promptly drove it into a ditch. Scholars cite the incident as the cataclysm that cleared the way for his rebirth as an art promoter.

Shipwreck became car accident.

74

By the time Marinetti had cast himself as the lead player in a worldwide troupe of innovative artists, manifesto publishing had become the standard vehicle for the introduction of all kinds of new schools of thought. Futurism proclaimed itself with a notice printed on the front page of Paris's *Le Figaro* on February 20, 1909. Over the next several decades, Futurism produced dozens of manifestos for the many threads of the movement that Marinetti claimed would bring about "global moral transformation."

Exactly what morals was a problem. Now regarded as the spear point of the avant garde in art—eclipsed in short order by cubism, vorticism, Dadaism, surrealism, and a host of other -isms—Futurism began with a rejection of tradition and a celebration of acceleration, but threw in dashes of violence and misogyny as well. Marinetti heralded war as "the world's only hygiene" and promised to destroy feminism. He published a novel, *Mafarka the Futurist*, that reads like Lucian playing Gilgamesh for one-liners. The conquering Mafarka-el Bar is more or less constantly on the rampage, raping slave girls who, once sated, tell the Nietzchean superman "you fill my little pussy's mouth with sugar and halva. It's happy to be so gorged on sweetmeats." The book was tried for obscenity three times.

Marinetti had a flair for attracting attention. He announced

Futurism in Paris with billboards, shouted slogans out taxi windows in Germany, sprinkled leaflets off clock towers in Venice. He recruited a range of thinkers and authors to draft Futurist manifestos on music, sculpture, lust, and fashion. Grand soirées, highly advertised evenings of readings and performances (in which the movement began to experiment with a new cuisine), were meant to provoke, annoy, and serve as the destructive force out of which a newly minted Futurist world would emerge. Pictures of Marinetti at the time—one part Hitler, one part Inspector Clouseau—perhaps explain why audiences sometimes walked out or lobbed firecrackers onstage.

Some Futurists were uncomfortable with Marinetti's glorification of violence; others complained that he had borrowed the

"ingredients" and a "recipe" for Futurism from France. World
War I arrived before anyone could stage a revolt. The Futurists,
Marinetti included, rushed off
to a conflict far more boring
than their romantic rhetoric
had suggested. Some left the
movement. Still, Futurism after the war reached its pinna-
cle of influence, beginning to
suggest utopian visions, a "new
Arcadia" with artists at the
helm. Some scholars deny that
Futurism ever amounted to a

true paradise because it did not offer up a plan for an ideal city.
In other words, eupsychia was not utopia. The criticism is un-
fair. The one Futurist who *had* designed a city—the author of
The Manifesto of Futurist Architecture—had been killed in the
war, shot in the head in 1916.

Futurism fell into bed early with Mussolini, though Marinetti later denounced fascism. In the midtwenties, Futurism
found itself folded into a global porridge of politics and art
movements. Marinetti fought to keep it alive and distinct. The
emphasis shifted from the automobile's speed to the perspective
of the airplane. All the manifestos were rewritten. *Manifesto of
Futurist Aeropainting, Manifesto of Aeropoetry, Futurist Manifesto of Aerial Architecture*. This last was another stab at a Futurist city, though by then it had flown somewhat beyond the pale:

> We Futurist poets, architects and journalists
> have conceived the great, unitary City as

made up of continuous lines to admire from the air, the parallel thrust of Aeroways and Aerocanals fifty meters wide, separated from one another by slender, materially and spiritually supplied habitations that will nourish all the diverse and distinct, never-intersecting speeds. The Aerostrade and the Aerocanale (which will unify rivers realigned in harmony with the airway lines) will transform the configuration of the plains, of the hills, and of the mountains.

By the thirties there were more Futurist manifestos being written than there were works of art inspired by them. Marinetti stayed true to his rhetoric. He again volunteered for military service in World War II. Past sixty, he served two years on the Russian front. He died in 1944.

75

But what of food?

Futurism slid into Italy's collective repressed memory. When historians returned to it in the sixties, questions nagged. Had futurism all been an elaborate scam? Was Marinetti's attempt to provoke a perfect world no different from More's wit, intended to chastise and wound? Was Marinetti utopian at all? And perhaps most important, did he like pasta?

A manifesto of Futurist cooking appeared as early as 1913, but late in Futurism's evolution Marinetti's interest in food and utopia returned with vigor. This time he drew on Fourier. He produced a series of articles on Futurist food in 1930, and *The Futurist*

Cookbook was published in 1932. From Fourier, Marinetti borrowed the idea that food could play a role in cultural rejuvena-
tion and a belief that pasta was not all it was cracked up to be.

As a pleasure prophet, Fourier had had a lot to say about food.
He noted that the most refined members of society were cooks
whose temperance permitted them access to "good cheer" without limit. Anticipating Maslow's good-choosing chickens, he
claimed that children and parents both could indulge without
fear of gluttony if only they became "refined gourmands." He
elaborated:

> If the whole human race could be raised to a
> high degree of gastronomic refinement, even
> in regard to the most ordinary kinds of foods,
> such as cabbages and radishes, and everyone
> be given a competence which would allow
> him to refuse all edibles which are mediocre
> in quality or treatment, the result would be
> that every cultivated country would, after a
> few years, be covered in delicious productions.

76

Surprisingly, pasta did not make the cut in Fourier's "associative phase."

Exogenous to Italy, which produces far more rice than wheat,
pasta was a utopian food product all on its own. A mayor of
Naples, where pasta had caught on in the seventeenth century,
proclaimed the fascination: "The Angels in Paradise eat nothing but vermicelli with tomato sauce." Yet the enthusiasm
expressed in some quarters was met with ire in others. A

Genoese doctor likened baskets of *trenette* to bags of coal in terms of digestibility. Fourier called pasta "rancid glue" that made the grocer rich. And Marinetti called for a pasta purge on the argument that it had made Italy a lugubrious nation. Plus, it was hard on the pancreas and the liver.

But Futurist cooking did not limit itself to a rant against the deadening effects of gluten. *The Futurist Cookbook* begins with a parable, "The Dinner That Stopped a Suicide," and a fictional Marinetti, even in brief summary, heroically expresses the goals of Futurist cuisine.

> Giulio, lovelorn Futurist, telegrams the famous aeropoet: "Immense sadness prevents my survival. Stop."
>
> Marinetti flies into action, recruiting two aeropainters to rush to his friend's aid.
>
> Giulio's self-diagnosis applies to all of Italy: "I sense your palates are bored with antiquated ways and I feel your belief that to eat like this is to prepare for suicide. . . . What do you advise?"
>
> The aeropoet advises transforming the kitchen into a fantastic laboratory.
>
> "To work, my aeropainters and aerosculptors! My aeropoetry will ventilate your brains like whirring propellers!"
>
> They create three edible golems, statues of beautiful women.
>
> The first is a "sculpted aerocomplex" of chestnut flour, eggs, milk, and cocoa, lacquered with a sugary down. Its creator warns his friends away.
>
> "You would eat her away from me without stopping for breath!"

The second is called The Passion of the Blondes and is made of puff pastry in descending pyramidal planes. Its chef is so awed by his own creation that he "tongue-kissed his work like a child."

The last is the masterpiece: The Curves of the World and Their Secrets. Equipped with cog-wheels, the figure animates when the men fall asleep. They wake to her chiding voice: "For pity's sake, you're like wild beasts. Control yourselves!"

Marinetti explains that the goal is to release the fugitive eternal feminine imprisoned in the stomach.

"You consider us wild. Others think us highly complicated and civilized."

When The Curves of the World and Their Secrets falls asleep in turn, the depressed Giulio kneels before it and begins to "adore it with his lips, tongue and teeth." He eats a foot, then heads for the "dense heart-of-heart pleasures." The feast liberates him, leaving him empty and bursting at once, "unique and complete."

The Futurist Cookbook proceeds with newspaper stories, accounts of soirées, and "formulas" for Futurist occasions. Marinetti proposed a Futurist Academy of Gastronomy and opened a restaurant dedicated to Futurist cuisine, the Holy Palate in Turin. The menu included dishes like Ultravirile ("designed for the ladies"), Elasticake ("cream in violent colors"), and Edible Landscape ("only for the gentlemen"). The new food was enabled by utopian innovation: *The Futurist Cookbook* anticipates a future filled with "featherweight aluminum trains," machines that constitute an "obedient proletariat," and meals that eschew nutritional concerns as daily nourishment is delivered Tesla-style via "nutritious radio waves."

77

But even before *The Futurist Cookbook* appeared, antagonists questioned Marinetti's utopian spirit, and even his indict-

ment of pasta. A photo was circulated in which Marinetti appeared to display reckless disregard for his pancreas, shoveling away a forkful of spaghetti. The futurist hoax was upended. As grainy as evidence of Bigfoot or Yeti, Marinetti claimed the image itself was the joke.

In retrospect, Marinetti had never looked like much of a kidder. But neither had Thomas More. What makes us laugh is tied to the world we live in. The comic is the first scrap of cultural detritus to wash down into history, and you can't tell the same joke twice. To all appearances celebrating technology and speed, Marinetti had called for "optimism at the table." Whatever he'd meant was long forgotten by the time DuPont borrowed the sentiment and offered a revision:

"Better living through chemistry." Not even Maslow's chickens took it for a punch line.

Parody became prophecy.

78

Clearly I needed to go to Italy. Italy un-got the joke of More before he even told it.

Marinetti aside, Italy was like a museum of utopian thought. Ancient social experiments conducted in the far south are counted as antiquity's most significant utopian trial runs, and Leonardo da Vinci's two-tiered city plans are just the tip of the iceberg of the culture's contribution to utopian city planning.* More modestly, it was the birthplace of a second food eupsychia, the Slow Food movement, which like Futurism sprouted up in Piedmont around a prominent personality, owed debts to France and communism, proposed a food university, drew on Fourier, and first announced its core ideas in a manifesto: the *Manifesto dello Slow Food*, first published in 1987.

Re-imagining the gastronome as a hybrid of Epicureanism and ecological conscience, Slow Food linked aesthetic taste to the taste of food, the painter's palette to the palate in your mouth. Slow Food wasn't really slow in the same way Futurist speed wasn't really fast. Rather, it was a kind of savoring, a combination of education and anticipation that echoed Fourier:

---

* *Utopia*'s King Utopus, modeled on Greek kings, is neatly matched by Italy's mythical founder, King Italus, whom Aristotle once credited with the introduction of common meals to the peninsula.

*in*conspicuous consumption, indulgence without excess. If Futurism had begun as a broad-ranging movement that imploded toward food as its influence waned, then Slow Food started with it and exploded: "Slow" philosophy had since been applied to everything that made the good life: Slow Beer, Slow Fish, Slow Sex, Slow Travel, Slow Design, Slow Cities.

In other words, psychology became place. Eupsychia became utopia.

And no one thought they were kidding. Slow Food launched immediately after the grand opening of the first McDonald's in Rome—i.e., as a response to *fast* food. The *Manifesto dello Slow Food* was another utopia attempting to repair dystopian damage caused by earlier utopias, a militant reply to the cataclysmic world that Futurism had helped to create.

> We are enslaved by speed and have all succumbed to the same insidious virus: Fast Life.... To be worthy of the name, *Homo Sapiens* should rid himself of speed before it reduces him to a species in danger of extinction.... Our defense should begin at the table with Slow Food.... Slow Food guarantees a better future.

79

In a country like a museum—as in a utopia—you need a good docent. I had a great one. As it happened, the significant adjacent cohabitator was a scholar of Italian legal history, a veteran of years of torturous research in the medieval archives of Florence. She came equipped with six languages over which she displayed a kind of proprietary pride (*my* Italian, *my* Greek, *my* medieval Latin legal shorthand, and so on), and she was engaged in a lifelong longitudinal study to upend established thinking on the origins of modern law. She *always* needed to go to Italy, and the idea to visit the birthplace of Slow Food was more hers than mine.

The cohabitator became docent.

80

Admittedly, our plan was incongruous.

We would land in Rome, and then rush to the far north to interview Slow Food's founder in Bra, near Turin. Then we would rush to a few of the founding towns of the Slow City movement, vaulting headlong through Italy and history but eating at certified Slow Restaurants all along the way. As a topper, we would rush to Rapallo on the Italian Riviera to attend a modern Futurist dinner.

Even if you cohabitate with someone significantly, I would argue, you don't really know them until you travel with them. It's like eating in that way. A dollop of romantic wisdom is implied in the conventional "dinner date": Watching someone eat offers insight into whether they will make an appropriate mate. Travel is the same. In terms of eating and travel both, the docent and I were a study in contrasts. A dichotomy. We knew that going in. In fact, the docent hoped that our trip would afford her opportunity—as she might phrase it—to civilize me. The docent was a gourmet cook and had been a card-carrying member of Slow Food for years. I was a child of Utopia Road, a suburb necropolis. For me, eating was no important ritual. Hunger was tribulation, trial. When I was hungry, the thing I wanted to be, as quickly as possible, was not hungry. I thought of astronaut food as a great innovation. Unwrap it, gobble it down. Nutritious radio waves? Even better.

The docent considered me a terminal case of the fast life.

Ah, but the docent was infected, too—a fact that didn't become apparent until we left for Rome. Travel with the docent was indeed "slow," but slow in this case meant—slow. As in tedious. As in inefficient. As in a belief that she was such a skillful packer of luggage that she could bring along everything she might ever need or desire, which of course meant that I wound up carrying far more than I would have had I traveled alone. It was even worse than that, actually. Any stop in our journey—security lines in airports being a prime example—was a chance for the docent to unpack one or two or all of her four carry-on items—the four carry-on items that she was certain fell within the traditional airline restriction of one carry-on item—and reorganize their contents on the fly. This reorganization process was entirely self-rewarding. It did not preclude further reorganizations (i.e., the bags were never "organized"), nor did it eliminate crises that arose from an inability to locate the proper item (tickets, keys, toiletries) at a moment of need. The important thing was to be perpetually engaged in a *regime* of reorganization. Which, to my mind, made it a characteristically post–information age dilemma: To be forever engaged in a hurried process of preparation, and to be so hurriedly preparing for future eventualities that you were not prepared for present realities, was to be unprepared, not to say disorganized. This failure of the idolization of multitasking and speed—leaving one harried and unable to carry one's own carry-ons—was yet another symptom of the fast life, dyspsychia, an ailment that slow philosophy was meant to combat.

But none of this, actually, prevented the docent and me from navigating, albeit with tribulation, the dome city dystopias of several international airports, slogging our way to the proper car rental desk, and slicking our way onto the proper auto-strada. Almost at once, it proved a wise choice to have acceded to the docent's slow plan: She offered keen insight into the Roman origin of the cultivation of cypress and umbrella pine trees, both prevalent along highways in central Italy, and she offered interesting observations on the Etruscan hill towns spackling Tuscany.* Italy was like being home again for the docent. A good portion of her identity had been formed when she was just twenty years old, here on scholarship, bumbling her way through the culture that would become her life's work. Now she charmingly regressed to that ardent postadolescent; she became bubbly and excited. She explained the games that we would play when we visited Florentine museums—Name that Saint and Find the Ugliest Baby Jesus—and I got the sense that Italy was alive for the docent precisely because she knew its history, from the Umbri and the Oscans down to Rome, and down further to the Goths and the Lombards and the city-states and the Medicis, and further still to Garibaldi

---

* The docent had once been seated at a communal dining table with Eric Newby and recognized him when he introduced his books' sidekick, his wife, Wanda. On learning her profession, Newby peppered the docent for Italian insight. Any guide good enough for the father of travel writing, I told myself, was good enough for me.

and Mussolini. This was slow history. To know something, to understand its origins, was to arrive at appreciation of it, to acquire a taste for it. The docent savored Italy, is perhaps the best way to say it, and for her it was a *stacked* affair. Without much room on the peninsula, she explained, civilizations had simply built on top of one another. It was this, I thought, that explained why Italy had failed to get the joke of *Utopia*. The book had been first translated into Italian by an itinerant doctor and a defrocked monk, and was published in Venice in 1548 with the decidedly unfunny title *The Newly Discovered Republic of the Government of the Isle of Eutopia.*

81

Which didn't exactly catch fire. The translation received mixed reviews. In 1553, it did inspire a treatise notable for its sober tone. "More stripped of ambiguities," one scholar described it. A compilation from 1561 demonstrated clearly that the joke had been lost: Utopia was listed alongside seventeen other societal systems, a few of which happened to be real. More's perfect commonwealth tickled no Italian funny bone because it was just another layer set atop a utopian spirit already well established in Italy. For years Florence had been thought a perfect system, and by the 1500s Venice had been an ongoing republic for eleven centuries, without internal strife and without ever falling to foreign rule. Now, borrowing More's template, utopias were written starring Venice as unironic protagonist. But more than for government or commune life, it was for architecture and city planning that Italy wished to applaud itself as utopia achieved, the *città felice* with avenues and piazzas inspired by the human form, the arteries and organs of a body politic. A body, it has since been observed, now sclerotic with traffic—the plentiful automobile Futurism had adopted as its emblem of paradise.

All of this was trundling through my mind as the docent and I rolled farther north in our own bit of rented plaque. I was happy. Central Italy looked a good bit like California— hence the spaghetti western—and I was pleasantly thinking back on times my brother, Peter, and I spent wandering the canyons around Utopia Road. As well, now that all of our carry-ons were secured, I had become significantly less anxious and dyspsychic and significantly more enamored of the docent. Indeed, I began to experience pleasant twinges of the typical utopian novel's adventurer-docent romantic subplot. Might not a little utopian role-playing, I wondered, wind up on our itinerary/menu? For her part, the docent became wistful. Her knowledge of Italy was stacked atop her personal experience of it, and she could not help but drip down into memory. Surprisingly, she expressed a desire to stop and take our first Italian meal at an Autogrill, the country's government-subsidized and wonderfully well-stocked chain of highway convenience stores. But this was not because she wanted to ease me slowly into the slow life. Rather, she admitted, it was because she had fond Autogrill memories with a previous significant cohabitator. Was this the same cohabitator, I wanted to know, with whom she'd had sex in every abandoned tower from here to the Po Valley? It was, in fact. The docent smiled vaguely, and with a casual flick of a hand identified a white streak on a distant mount as the site where Michelangelo had quarried his marble.

We didn't arrive in Bra until after dark. It was a handsome three-story medieval downtown, gray and noirish, with shadows and sharp angles and three churches that sounded the hour at different times with bells gone flat from age. We pulled into the piazza of our B&B, close to all the Slow Food businesses that had sprouted up around the organization's offices. The docent raved about the three-hundred-year-old door to our room and the five-hundred-year-old beam holding up our ceiling. The twelve-hour flight and ten-hour drive had been a frenzied dash, but now we decelerated. Out for a stroll, the docent smiled at signs marking Renaissance urban territories and said, "Welcome to my world."

We stopped at a bar for a liqueur. On the way back we passed one of the churches, and the docent had a rule: Enter every open church you pass in Italy. Inside it was cold and cavernous, saints huddled in alcoves like hibernating bears. We moved forward in faint votive light. There were two women in the pews. After a moment one of them rose and moved deeper into the sanctuary. The hour sounded above us in its sad key, and it wasn't until the fourth or fifth chime that I glimpsed the woman's back, straining with the pulls.

"That woman is *ringing* the bells."

"Of course she is," the docent said.

82

Slow Food began with a course of overdone thrushes and a *ribollita* cooked too quickly for too many people.

In 1982, one-time Communist politician Carlo Petrini was looking to learn a thing or two about wine. Head of a troupe of friends from Bra that dabbled in politics and food—they ran a small radio station called Red Waves and operated a co-op grocery—Petrini had managed to get himself elected to the town's mostly conservative city council in the seventies, only to resign a short time later in a scandal over earthquake relief funds. It hadn't been a good time to be on the Italian Left. The country was swinging in the other direction, and some had resorted to violence—terrorism—in reply. Petrini and his friends turned to food instead. In 1980, they formed an association that organized tasting courses to create awareness for local products. Their goal was community for food, with wine culture as a model. But they didn't know wine, so they set out on a variety of trips—mainly north, to France—to give themselves an education in taste. This same education would years later be written into the mission statement of Slow Food's University of Gastronomic Sciences, just outside Bra.

One journey the friends took—south, in 1982—amounted to a turning point. Curious about the Brunello di Montalcino, the first wine to receive Italy's state seal of approval, they arranged to attend Montalcino's Festival of the Thrush, an annual communal feast. The festival organizers were Communists, too, but it turned out that the distance between Bra and Montalcino amounted to more than a six-hour drive. There was a sharp line separating brands of Italian Communist: Those from the north found southerners too ascetic; those from the south found northerners too French.

In other words, the meal was awful. The thrushes were ruined, the *ribollita* was botched. The wine was too cold, and even the service was terrible. The friends were so distressed they penned a letter of complaint.

Dear Comrades . . .

We are of the firm opinion that the preparation
and serving of food is a serious enterprise. To
be sure, at political banquets one has to be prepared to suffer a stomachache in the service of
one's beliefs. . . . However, we think we have
had enough with comrades who act as cooks or
as waiters. . . . We know nothing of the budget
of Montalcino, yet undoubtedly that hideous
meal on Sunday earned you something. . . . If
we treated our members here like that we'd be
publicly lynched, we'd be considered not comrades anymore, but rather filthy reactionaries,
fascists. . . . We felt the urge to tell you this because we hope that you will give up acting like
restaurateurs before someone finally files a
claim for damages.

The swift reply was a challenge.

Dear Comrades,

Eleven different tours with 530 people visited
our circle, and I can assure you that 515 guests
(i.e., everybody but you) were enthusiastic
about their experience here. . . . I could go on
by telling you about the activities of our circle, but I believe that it would be much better
to discuss it openly. To this end, I am thinking about organizing a debate here in Montalcino, to compare our perspectives and
experiences. . . .

Petrini jumped at the chance. When the debate was
conducted—actually, an effort to put him on trial—he came

into his own as a food crusader. He won over hostile crowds with the argument that it was time for the Left to pay as much attention to food as to party enrollment.

Slow Food had found its visionary but needed a few years to simmer yet. The friends continued their education. A pair of events in March 1986, gave their message perspective and an enemy. Nineteen deaths resulting from methanol-spiked wine proved that attention paid to the relationship between food producers and consumers was about more than fancy dinners, and McDonald's opening a restaurant near the Spanish Steps announced the formal invasion of the fast life.

Outrage over the Big Mac matched that for the lethal Barbera. Petrini staged protests armed with bowls of penne. The restaurant chain replied in kind.

"We intend to conquer Italy," said the president of McDonald's Development Italy.

83

The conflict gave the movement its metaphor. If McDonald's was fast, they would be slow. The *Manifesto dello Slow Food* appeared a short time later, and the Bra-based organization looked no farther than the next town over, Cherasco, home of the edible snail, for its symbol and logo. The launch of the movement included a grand soirée in Paris timed to coincide with press conferences on five continents.

Publishing fueled rapid growth. Slow Food compiled lists of inns and restaurants that valued tradition, used local products, and did not reserve good taste for special occasions or deep pockets. The guidebooks that resulted sold hundreds of thousands of copies, enabling further slow endeavors. The first of these was the Ark of Taste.

Petrini took his lead from Lévi-Strauss, whose *The Raw and the Cooked* argued that the emergence of culture was linked to cooking (nature/culture=raw/cooked), and now, Petrini claimed, that same culture was subject to an annihilation "unprecedented in human history." The goal of the Ark of Taste was to find and preserve foods and flavors threatened by the fast life—industrialization. Petrini was dubbed the "Noah of Bra," and the Ark came to include suborganizations called "presidia" that worked to generate business for specific threatened products.

The movement offered a new philosophy: ecogastronomy. Alimentary knowledge was as important as reading and writing, Petrini wrote, but the gastronome who blindly indulged was "yesterday's man." Slow Food's membership swelled to eight thousand in three years, reached twenty thousand in the early nineties, and topped eighty thousand after the turn of the century. The success emboldened Petrini. He planned a worldwide network of underrepresented farmers, "food communities" linked through advances in communications technology, a network that could push back against the isolation of the fast life. The first Terra Madre was held in 2004, 4,800 people from 1,200 food communities in 130 countries gathering in Turin for a kind of United Nations of food. Workshops fostered exchanges of techniques and values.

Petrini glowed in the aftermath: "When we start to lose the feeling of being alone . . . and we are able to work in the name of our community of destiny, no business, no change, no machine will be able to stop our quest for happiness."

84

I was skeptical about Slow Food. And I was annoyed when Petrini was late for our scheduled interview.

The docent and I were ushered into his office to wait after a morning spent touring the University of Gastronomic Sciences. The school was housed in a converted country estate with Roman floors and cellars preserved beneath transparent flooring. Weary students packed food technology classrooms. It was not a cooking school, they took pains to tell us. Slow Food was not for chefs.

Of Petrini, our escort said, "He's never cooked a meal in his life! Don't tell him I told you that."

Which sort of explained my skepticism. I was getting used to the idea that earnest utopians—Paul Martin, Kat Kinkade, Knut Kloster Jr.—were figures of romantic tragedy. Petrini was anything but tragic. His office featured three shelves of snail idols, trinkets accumulated over a quarter century of prosperous growth. The effort to mythologize him was ongoing. His mother had birthed him, one story said, with the help of a midwife whose name was the Italian word for glutton. He had never stepped foot inside a fast-food restaurant, it was claimed, nor could he remember having eaten a packaged snack. He had recently been identified by the *Guardian* as one of fifty people in the world who might be able to save the planet.

Which was odd because Petrini was also one of those utopians who bristled at the utopian label. This had annoyed me further. Or pre-annoyed me. In any event, in preparing for our interview I had pored through his books, dog-earing those spots where he used utopia himself. I intended to corner him with his own words.

He arrived finally with an entourage of friends, bringing with him a just-released video documentary about a manioc flour farmer from the Amazon who had attended the second Terra Madre, which in 2006 drew twice as many participants as the first. We watched the video there in the office, a heart-felt fish-out-of-water story celebrating food producers who still packed their product in leaves and handmade baskets.

We rearranged the seating for our interview. Petrini was a boisterous man with a splatter of beard and a loud laugh, a back-clapper of a guy. The docent was a little in awe of him. She translated tentatively until I nudged her and asked her to speak up for the tape recorder. We were interrupted by repeated phone calls, more visitors, and a moment of confusion over the questions I had designed to expose the utopian dimensions of Slow Food.

My plan failed. Petrini offered the most lucid defense of utopian thought I had so far encountered.

85

Here is what he said:

"We seek to enjoy food not only at the sensory level, but also at full appreciation and knowledge of it. Knowing the producer, knowing the mode of production, knowing that the mode of production does not destroy the environment, allows you to take greater pleasure in whatever you consume. Intellectual, sensory, and political knowledge of food. A person who seeks to enjoy something through sensory perception alone is not a person of good taste.

"I went to France to gain a greater appreciation of the experience of wine. But even that approach is limiting—it's not enough. Because it doesn't take into account the environmental destruction of traditional methods. One cannot be a gastronome if one is concerned with pleasure only outside the context of the attendant risks of food production. Thus our slogan: 'A gastronome who isn't an environmentalist is an idiot. And an environmentalist who isn't a gastronome is a very sad man.'

"Utopian socialism could be revived. It's not that there's no life in it. It can be resuscitated—because it's an ideology of hope. The message of Marx and Engels was applied to the fruits of a nascent industrial society. We live in a postindustrial society—a postmodern society. The industrial production mode has broken the connection between humanity and nature. Marx and Engels offered a vision opposed to capitalism. They thought capitalism would arrive at a point where the proletariat would break their bonds of servitude, gain control. But it never happened because capitalism changed, evolved. It became global. Instead of the proletariat breaking their chains, the workers assisted the system in destroying nature. Humanity is no longer a confrontation of classes. For the first time in history, we face together the dilemma of our existence. We're at the brink of extinction—and that's the difference.

"Food guarantees our survival. The relationship between humans and food has always been *the* relationship of central importance. All cultures, all religions recognize food as one of the sacral elements, the central staple item. We waste a great deal of energy today creating very mediocre food. A higher quality product may actually require less energy in its production. A simple way to do this is to eat according to the seasons. Another is to relocalize production. These things guarantee higher quality in terms of freshness, and we wind up spending far less money on pesticides, refrigeration, chemical preservation, etc. Because *these* modes of production are principally responsible for the destruction of ecosystems and biodiversity, we need to consider change. If we don't change these destructive methods, we risk loss of soil, loss of water, loss of all biodiversity on Earth. If the world suffers, we also suffer.

"I want to be an optimist. I have faith in the possibilities of the future, even if today we are preoccupied with notions of degeneration. So we send out our battalions to fight for an optimistic cause, a right cause, a just cause. You can say many things about the concept of utopia—especially that it's a bad idea. But it is necessary to cultivate, a bit, the notion of a utopia. To be a visionary. Utopian visions carry us forward. These visions find concrete forms, transform hope into reality. It is necessary that we put faith in the idea that change can occur."

86

We had made our journey in January, which was both the best and the worst time to visit Italy. Many businesses were closed, but those open year-round catered to a clientele of actual Italians, a rarity in Italy, the docent said. The following morning we pushed open our blinds to another rarity—a perfect inch of snow fallen all across the city.

We went to Cherasco for snails. It was one of those moody hilltop towns, founded in the thirteenth century, still ready to go it alone as it once had. We had wine and olives at a local bar and discovered a church facade whose memorial stones the docent could read as geologists read sediment. Americans fixate on the art of Italy, she said, the architecture, the food. Yet the political advances we attribute to ourselves—with a nod to Rome or Greece—formed in northern Italy five hundred years before the Founding Fathers. The city-state, mercantile capitalism. Commune cities in the Val di Fiemme first gave women the right to vote in 1173. History is recorded in the stones.

She was ready for a utopian meal. She cracked our menu that night at a Cherasco *trattoria* and cried slow, happy tears. We had local wine and first courses of a flaky tuna with capers that burned the roof of the mouth, rabbit like gamey fowl, and a potato gnocchi held together by surface tension alone, delicate as a soap bubble. The world's great clockwork was already creaking, but it wasn't only the food that set the docent off—it was the simple room and the sense that for the young couple across from us, out for perhaps their second or third date, the meal was ontological indulgence, the restaurant neither sanctuary nor ceremony, but home. The room filled in with a family of five, two pairs of elderly couples, and a large gathering of young professionals, the men on one side with beer, the women across from them with wine. It was the old and young gathered together that charmed the docent, a demonstration of the etymological similarity of cultural and culinary. I took a less ethnographic view: Dinner in Italy was all about staring. Italians appeared to love staring—either staring themselves or being the subject of staring. They stared shamelessly. I myself stared at a man all through our course of hand-folded ravioli, while he in turn stared at a young lady with what might be termed gray-scale audacity. It was not lewd; it was study. It was prelapsarian trance state. Italy did not need a promised land of milk and honey, or a Bengodi, or a Land of Cockaigne, because it had never fallen out of paradise to begin with.

In utopian literature it is often the case that the protagonist adventurer, in beholding the splendor of the paradise upon which he has stumbled, is at some point left to reflect on his own poor culture, his home. That's the whole point of utopian novels—at least, the ironic ones. And that's what I did now, as we moved on to our snails, bathed in butter and oil, and our celery and cheese salad. The food of the fast life drove people apart, I thought, into "family restaurants" (which described the menu better than the clientele), pizza joint theme parks (where suburban children constituted a new street urchin), and fast-food franchises that operated like banks or gas stations (often alongside them). Food was shame in the fast life. Food was chore, food was budget item, game show, pornography, sin. My first slow meal was a fast lesson in disgrace, a glimpse of a hollow within myself that had triggered no corresponding hunger.

"You're doing pretty good at eating slowly," the docent said. "It must be killing you."

We finished with a flan and a grappa that scoured the body's plumbing. We stayed longer than the elderly couples, not as long as the young lovers. As we fell asleep that night, the docent whispered Latin plural forms in my ear, caressing my calf with her toes.

87

Eupsychian Management: "Finally, one consequence of this article is an increased emphasis on slowness of social change, even of necessary slowness. We must have the patience of the scientist who waits until the data are in before he draws his conclusions."

88

The snails did not sit well. The docent didn't care. Taking her morning constitutional, she sang, "Here comes the snail!" to the tune of *Flight of the Valkyries* (it works in Italian), and after strategically reorganizing all the socks and stockings in her carry-ons ("I'm doing this for your benefit"), she conducted an impromptu puppet show to decide which of them to wear for our drive to Levanto.

We drifted through the Po region, piercing thick mists like the snow cover changing its mind and heading back into the sky, and passing forests of poplar in rows, files, diagonals: tree farms lifted from the pages of *Utopia*. Levanto was on the coast and had been recommended to us as a model Slow City. It was a cove town, a tight urban space pressed up against a tiny harbor, a stone quay facing the water. The hills above town—behind it— were filled with *frazzioni*, tiny hamlets that together formed a collective olive farm. There were two presidia here—one for a species of unattractive lemon that suffered by comparison to the handsome Amalfi lemon and one for a local anchovy that Roman soldiers had used as provision but was now being pushed out by industrial fish farming. Levanto had retained a barter culture until the 1960s; it was one of those places where salt had been used as money. Just north of the Cinque Terra, the town had been effectively cut off from Italy until Mussolini made the trains run on time. The University of the Gastronomic Sciences had sent students to Levanto to study local production methods, and when the Slow City movement formed in 1999 the town quickly applied for membership, agreeing to adhere to a variety of slow standards in exchange for Slow City status, which attracted slow tourists using slow guides to find slow restaurants. Like us.

Except there weren't any. At least not in January. We hiked a kilometer from our inn down into town, spent some time sitting on the quay, where Italians approached their afternoon strolls with a sense of civic duty and indulged in a lot more shameless staring, visited the *enoteca* where Petrini was revered in local minds, climbed the endless stairs to the local castle, and then attempted to make reservations at the local slow restaurant, only to discover that Sunday afternoon in January was perhaps the worst possible time to be trying to give your business to ecologically minded restaurateurs. We wound up eating in a restaurant that might as well have been an Italian restaurant in Eau Claire, Wisconsin, with checkerboard tablecloths, farm implement wall decor, and tart wine. The anchovies were fine, but the gnocchi were a rubbery remnant of the fast life, foam pellets sponging up a sauce that rasped of the tin

it had come in. The bilingual menu was the first bad sign, and
the docent sighed deeply when she spotted the notice fessing
up to the use of frozen vegetables. It was early; we ate alone.
Halfway through our meal, our waitress cracked the door to a
shady-looking fellow who gave her a small package in exchange
for a handful of euros. The waitress stuffed the package into
the pocket of her apron and returned to our table. More
wine?

We agreed that it was a forgettable meal and tried to forget
it, but the problem with forgettable meals is that you don't
forget them. They fester. The docent's mood was spoiled, and
it only got worse when we returned to our slow inn. She
wanted to go to Florence, she said. The problem was that
while it had been the docent's idea to slow tour Italy, I had
made all the plans and reservations. The last thing she wanted
to be in Italy was a tourist, and that's what we were doing,
touring, slowly, it was true, but quickly slowly, and that was
my fault. What she would prefer was Florence, where it wasn't
safe, but at least she could lock herself in the archives and
work. History is the refuge of failed dreamers. The docent
hadn't paid her Slow Food dues in years. I tried to cheer her up
with a list of Italy's contemporary utopian innovations: the
radiators that doubled as towel warmers, the lights all on tim-
ers, the policy of tunneling through mountains for roads instead of decapitating them. It didn't help. The docent was
working on her computer now, attempting to uncorrupt some
files that had become corrupted, some files that she needed for
her work in the archives, but she couldn't uncorrupt them, and
I was to blame, because here we were vaulting around Italy,

and it was all too fast, too headlong, didn't I know that, no I didn't, and she was angry with me, and it was a waste of time, and her life had been a waste, hadn't it, and what was I doing wasting her time, corrupting her, with stupid projects and bad food?

89

It got worse overnight. The docent woke to a dyspsychian mood. She even turned on Petrini; she wasn't convinced Slow Food was more than affectation.

"Eighty-six thousand people are not going to convince billions to stop eating fast food, to stop wanting everything to be as easy as possible. You can't do it. You can't stop the loss of species. A farmer packing his flour in leaves is a dying way of life. There's nothing to be done. There's nothing to be done."

Sunday in January was the worst possible time for slow touring Italy—with the possible exception of Monday. It would be our day of frustrations. I talked the docent out of Florence for the time being, and we headed south into Chianti. Bra had been one of the four original slow cities, and Greve in Chianti was another, but when we got to Greve it was empty, the town was on vacation, the slow *trattorie* and *osterie* and *locande* were all either closed for the season, or open for the season but closed on Mondays, and by then our rented plaque was acting up, and we had to pay twenty euros to a local mechanic who looked in the engine compartment and shrugged, because it wouldn't misbehave for him. We hit the road again, following the advice of the slow guide to head deeper into Chianti, but the cell signal grew dim and we couldn't call the inns that were open, and a slow restaurant we tried for lunch was closed even though it was supposed to be open. We got hungry. The plaque began misbehaving again. The docent had pointed out the charming little three-wheeled motorcarts that Italians used for local hauling—*api*, bumblebees—but now the *api* were passing us on the charmingly annoying winding roads of Chianti.

"We've got a bumblebee on our ass," the docent said, squinting at the rearview mirror and squeezing the steering wheel to punish it. "This car has all kinds of opinions."

I was frantically paging through the slow guide because the afternoon was rolling along and we had nowhere to stay for the night, and my stomach was rolling along now, too, because I was reading while the docent was driving, and though the docent was a good driver in some respects—as a conversationalist while driving, for example—she could have used a remedial course or two in steering and braking, a certain tentativeness in each compounding the annoying windiness of Chianti's roads. We settled on Gaiole in Chianti to stay for the night, which we could reach by cell but was another hour's drive off, an hour in which hunger was compounded by nausea, and by disappointment because there was a slow inn in Gaiole, but no slow restaurant. Frustration gave way to despondency, and we steeled ourselves—to the extent it is possible to be despondent *and* steeled—for the likelihood that the sad day would end with another poor meal. I had the fleeting thought that if I had not been spoiled with good food, if I had not slowed down from the fast life, then a quick bite on the fly, even in Italy, would not have seemed so much like defeat.

We steeled ourselves, too, for the likelihood that Gaiole would disappoint, though it turned out to be an entirely charming town. We were hungry, but we took a walk as a way of procrastinating, as a way of delaying the disappointing meal we anticipated. Gaiole was a one-piazza town. It was both old and new. The church was new, but the stone houses were old. As it was the worst possible time to be traveling in Italy, we were the only ones doing it. However, it was precisely because it was the worst time to be traveling in Italy that it was possible, in a small wine town routinely overrun with tourists in the summer, to get a sense of what it might actually be like to live in such a place and not just visit. In other words, we were able to appreciate Gaiole, we were able to savor its slowness. We strolled slowly through the market. The Italians were doing their vegetable shopping. All the vegetables were marked with placards indicating where in Italy they had grown. They were fresh and bright. We walked through the town playground, next to the elementary school. The church bells chimed the end of band practice. A gang of school kids appeared, and for a moment we were surrounded by children with undersized instruments in undersized instrument cases. One boy tooted out a slow melody on his tiny trumpet, and was accompanied by an overexcited puppy out for a stroll before dinner. Like us.

The charming town charmed us, but we had no hopes beyond that. Our innkeeper recommended a restaurant up the road, but it wasn't in the slow guide, so how good could it be? We went anyway; it was dark; we were hungry. The parking lot was empty, but the lights were on. The docent stepped inside to see if they were open. She returned, sour but resigned.

"They're open, but they look *young*."

A young woman seated us; we were the only customers. She left us alone with the menus and stayed away long enough that it was natural to wonder whether the service was slow or non-existent. No matter—the menu was interesting, both because it wasn't translated and because of what it said. The docent explained that the dishes were broken into two categories, traditional and creative, and she was tickled and intrigued by the description of a wine that "finish[ed] with a discrete and succinct persistence." She kept repeating the phrase, discrete and succinct persistence, and we tried to taste the persistence when it came, which wasn't hard to do, we agreed, because the description was accurate. Without realizing it, we had become happy again—as a function of patience and persistence. The salad—artichoke, Parmesan, cabbage, arugula—made us happier still, and less hungry. I had soup of a local bean, creamed and simple, and the docent ate a grain that had first been cultivated in Italy in 7000 BC. We ate slowly. The docent approved. "You're not American anymore," she told me. "You're not Italian, but you're not American either." We palate-cleansed with San Pellegrino and traded spoonfuls of soup and grain as Nat King Cole, slow and timeless and warm, crept out from the kitchen along with the sounds of cooking and of laughter. After a time, our *secondi* arrived, white meatballs and wild asparagus—local pork and a winter vegetable. We ate guiltlessly and stared at each other shamelessly.

The restaurant itself was both old and new, both timeless and warm. Our young waitress, who was actually the young co-owner of the restaurant, explained that the structure was medieval, and that for several centuries it had been a forge, servicing the local castle. After the forge closed, it had been an antique store for more than a century. The young co-owner and her husband, the young chef, had earned the patronage of the Swiss owner of the castle and more than four hundred local investors, so that now the restaurant was a co-op set atop the hollow of the old oven. The young chef came to sit with us. We were still their only customers. They had been cooking and laughing all night. If you are truly a restaurateur, they explained, then the restaurant is your home, and they preferred a home that, like their food, paid a debt to the past even as it spoke to contemporary life. They had been inspired by Catherine de' Medici, who introduced gastronomy to France and, by some accounts, invented the fork. Their goal was tranquility, and a rhythm of dining. She was twenty-seven; he was twenty-nine.

Their names were Diego and Valentina. And this was so wonderful, so charming, that for days I found myself whispering the two names in the shower, Diego and Valentina, Diego and Valentina, surely the kinds of names that Shakespeare would have jotted into a notebook. Diego and Valenina. I looked at the docent. I wished that *our* names were Diego and Valentina. The docent smiled back in a way she had of smiling, a broad, intentional proclamation of satisfaction—a eupsychian smile. It wasn't heaven, but the world did seem better for a moment or two. I sipped my grappa; it left me hollow and full, empty and bursting at once.

Dinner lasted four hours.

90

Our slow luck continued the following day. Todi was another Slow City, another walled hilltop town. Our room was a Bohemian apartment high up in the tiered peak of mossy rooftops. A small terrace looked out across the misty valley, where it was raining, though we were higher than the clouds, higher than the rain, and we could admire it from above, a white chill sheet hugging the city all around. The room had a kitchenette and a fireplace and cheesy art and creaky furniture and the docent loved it.

"I could live with you here. For a year. If I had to."

We spent the afternoon hiking Todi's cobbled streets, up and down private walks to private dead ends, the doors of homes opening directly onto the streets so that the whole place had the feel of a single home, the roads like corridors of a larger enclosure—a phalanstery, perhaps. The docent cried again at the tomb of Jacopone de' Todi under the San Fortunata church—he was one of the poet jurists critical to her archival work—and she thrilled at some of the church's art, specifically a particularly ugly baby Jesus, but dismissed a lot of it as tripe, which was tricky to do in Italy because tripe—bovine stomach lining—was a traditional food product, a local delicacy. Back outside, the city was alive with people doing their afternoon shopping, babies crying, water prickling along beneath grates in the street.

"So can you imagine medieval gangs roaming around slitting one another's throats at night?"

"Pretty creepy in the dark, huh?"

Walled cities evolved without internal police forces, the

docent explained. The city-state formed as collective self-protection; safety provided the opportunity for the emergence of a sophisticated system of internal jurisprudence.

"You can't have self-governance without leisure."

Our leisurely dinner that night included goose, wild boar, and venison sausages, dried fish–stuffed tomatoes, and a chickpea and mushroom soup. I had tripe. We were joined again by the establishment's owner, a sixtyish man named Fabio who had worked in the large animal feed business before attending a Slow Food dinner some years before. He invested in the *locanda* so that his wife, Loredana, could put the cooking skills she had inherited and honed to good use. Fabio and Loredana. Fabio explained that food in the region had deteriorated in the sixties, when locals began to hunger for goods and technology. Technology was a sign of prosperity, of entering the global community. In most places, like Florence, the literal walls had come down long before, and in the sixties the figurative walls fell even in places like Todi. The fast life streamed in. F. T. Marinetti may have been kidding but no one in Todi was laughing.

"Futurism was a mistake," Fabio said. "Marinetti was wrong. It didn't used to be this way—now everything is stress. Marinetti's vision did not happen in the twenties. It happened in the sixties."

91

But it was wrong to conclude, then, that Slow Food, or slow philosophy, was antiglobalization or antitechnology, a point that had been made to us in Bra and was reiterated the next day in Orvieto, our final Slow City. Orvieto was yet another hilltop town, and we rode up to it in an elevator whose shaft passed through an Etruscan water pipeline, which, we were told, was a good example of how the modern could recycle the ancient, how the old and new could complement each other. We headed for Orvieto's Palace of Taste. All Slow Cities had a Palace of Taste—Orvieto's was another food school in a converted monastery—and we were met there by the head of Cittaslow International, a man named Oliveti, who explained how the Slow City movement differed from the Slow Food movement. It was a shift from organizing private members to public organs, a change in rationale from ethical indulgence to indulgence in ethic. Slow philosophy was itself a form of globalization,  he said, a worldwide effort at ethical self-governance. The Slow City movement had grown at a leisurely pace.

There were now about fifty Slow Cities, in places like Spain and Poland and Australia, all of them self-governing for energy usage, waste disposal, recycling standards, and so on.

The docent liked Oliveti so much I heaved a sigh of relief that there were no abandoned towers in Orvieto. There was a duomo, however. The docent had what might be termed gray-scale affinity for duomos. I had tried arguing that the Middle Ages were well mapped out by either food or utopias—Athenaeus and Catherine de' Medici on the one hand, Plato and More on the other—but the docent preferred duomos: Hadrian's Pantheon in Rome and Brunelleschi's Basilica di Santa Maria del Fiore in Florence. The duomo in Orvieto, she said, had something we could not miss: the frescoes of Luca Signorelli depicting the end of the world—paradise and hell.

It was the birth of perspective, the docent said. Not to mention the fact that Signorelli had depicted the blessed as naked for the first time in an age. The Renaissance return to paradise had begun; Italy lost its medieval shame. We stared at the frescoes. The docent nodded up to the artist's self-portrait, in a corner. Had I noticed that his was the only figure in the whole work looking back at us? Unheard of. Art in the Middle Ages wasn't even signed. I noticed it now—and I noticed the docent was wrong.

The ugly baby Jesus was staring at us, too.

92

We spent a couple of days in Florence. The docent disappeared into the archives; I got cheated on a leather sport coat in the Piazza San Lorenzo. We returned the rented plaque, and on Friday we took a train to Rapallo.

The man who had arranged a Futurist dinner for us maintained a rough-hewn look. Apart from his Futurist costume of bowler hat, red tie, black vest, and glasses low on his nose, he might have looked content hunched over a wooden puppet,

chiseling in the details. His name was Donati. His wife, Myriam, was Basque. They met us in the lobby of the Hotel Eu-
ropa, a grand spectacle that had once catered to the likes of
Pound, Eliot, Hemingway, and D'Annunzio. Donati had been
asked to write a history of the hotel a few years before, and newspaper accounts of its golden age introduced him to Futurism—
not taught in Italian schools, he told us. He had since launched a
movement to reconfigure Futurism for its hundredth anniversary the following year. So far he had just a handful of artists
onboard.

A local restaurant had agreed to host the dinner, and Donati had been helping with the six-course meal all day. He met
us an hour before the first course was to be served, but had
only a few minutes for an interview before he had to return to
the kitchens. Perhaps I didn't like Donati because he seemed
rushed. Perhaps because he seemed too eager to please. Or
perhaps I could already sense that in a few months' time he
would cheat the docent on the price of a translation she would
do for him. In any event, I felt compelled to pressure him on
the logic of resurrecting a movement that rejected anything
old.

"Marinetti hated tradition," I said, "yet you look back on
the tradition of Marinetti."

"No. The dynamics of this movement do not have chrono-
logical limits. The contents are very different."

"How?"

"The methodology is basic. Confront reality, and escape academia. Free oneself of the canon. But the content today does not
need to be the same. We don't have to exult in machines, or

trains—they are not the objects of our culture. We could exult in missiles, or other things."

"So you're looking to the future."

"Yes, of course. But in the sense of the complete artist who expresses himself in all camps. That's a utopia. It's as in the Renaissance, when the ideal was the universal man and you were expected to do and know all things. It was a culture built on an epistemological foundation. The grand message of Futurism is that culture is a unity."

He had to get back to dinner.

The docent and I returned to our room upstairs, with its blind doors and marble windowsills and shuttered views looking across yet another cove town, this one tricked up like Miami with haughty pastel awnings and a fleet of sailboats in the harbor. We went for a walk. We couldn't decide whether it was a good idea to go to a Futurist dinner hungry. The slow guide bragged of a slow restaurant somewhere in Rapallo—in particular its rabbit stew and herb salad—though by the time I thought to look it up we were late for Donati's restaurant.

My leather jacket was nothing compared to the suits and gowns of the two other couples in our party, wealthy retirees dressed for the twenties in jewels and waxed mustaches. We were seated near the restaurant's kitchen, alongside a multimedia console. Donati had prepared a slideshow of Futurist art and had collected snippets of recording and film. Dinner would be punctuated by Futurist poetry read by Myriam, but it began with a recording of Marinetti himself. Futurist poetry emphasized the onomatopoetic. The poems looked like

eye exam charts, and Marinetti's delivery was a hybrid of scat
and Mussolini's maniacal oration. It was prelanguage poetry,
it was pre-aural imagination; it was nearly prenatal. When it
was her turn, Myriam read Futurist poems like a mother trying to impress an infant of already refined taste.

93

The first course was an aperitif of Marinetti's own design. It
was called *Inventina*, meaning study or composition, and the
orange-twanging liqueur was the most palatable thing of the
whole meal. It rendered the docent useless as a translator, and
she spent much of the rest of the night giggling or pushing
food around on her plate, pretending to eat. The Intuitive
Antipasti included anchovies and mushrooms stuffed inside
whole orange peels, several slices of sausage, and a wedge of
raw butter. This was followed by *Traidue*, three-two, attributed to an aeropainter and consisting of toast, apple chunks,
and strips of more sausage, and *Decola-paladar*, decapitated
palate, a soup of equal parts meat broth and brandy, with rose
petals.

The Futurist poetry caught the attention of the restaurant
staff and those Italians there simply to eat. The waiters ignored
us, but the patrons seemed hostile. Even the chef, who came out
to greet us, fessed up to mixed feelings about the affair because
the restaurant's owners were Neapolitan and Marinetti had rid-
iculed Neapolitan culture mercilessly. Donati was thrilled. The
other two couples in our party assumed an air of bemused indif-
ference.

If the problem with forgettable meals was that they could not be forgotten, then the goal of Futurist cuisine was to be so forgettable as to be indelible. Dinner continued with Surprised Sausage Under First Snow with Spinach Zig Zag (hot dogs, mashed potatoes, spinach) and concluded with the Breasts of Saint Agatha (two scoops of ice cream strategically topped with cherries). But it was the main course that brought it together for me, that betrayed the joke of Futurist cuisine once and for all. Marinetti's food influence had not stopped with Fourier or France or Paul Adam—it returned, as had his dystopian play, to the Land of Cockaigne. In the tens of thousands of versions of the poem that razed the continent, a constant was the mythical land's edible architecture. Fences of sausage, doors and windows of salmon and sturgeon, butter roof beams, meat-pie furniture, pastry rooftops, streets paved with spices. The whole place was edible. Medieval courts had not been content to just read about it. Peculiar dinners were organized in which the consumption of food played second fiddle to its arrangement, delicacies molded into moving forms that acted out battles and sieges—and shipwrecks. Futurist cuisine was built atop the efforts to realize Cockaigne; Marinetti had recycled the ancient. Our main course arrived on giant silver platters. Architectonic Plate of Sant'Elia, The Bombing of Adrianopolis, and Carneplastico. This last was a monolithic cylindrical meatloaf positioned alongside vertically thrusting fruit kebabs of banana, strawberry, and cherry, and a large dome mold of something that ought never to have been gelled. The point was not to disgust us—but I had to be disgusted to realize it. I tried the gelatin. It gripped my tongue like cellophane and triggered some kind of reverse swallow reflex. I tasted it twice. Donati was smiling; I hated him and his poetry. I leaned back in my chair.

And then I saw it—our dinner in profile, in miniature. It was a skyline. The food was a city; the city was food.

A CITY

*When he enters the territory of which
Eutropia is the capital, the traveler sees not
one city but many, of equal size and
not unlike one another, scattered over
a vast rolling plateau.*

—ITALO CALVINO,
Invisible Cities

*When these communities find their proper
historian, who comes not to mock but rather
to understand, the image of the utopian
and his ideal society may be
significantly amended.*

—FRANK MANUEL,
Utopian Thought in the Western World

94

By March 2000, Dr. Jay Kim was in a bit of a bind.

It was a weird job to begin with: Find an American developer for a master-planned city and international business district (IBD) in a free economic zone (FEZ) on an artificial island the Korean government "reclaimed" on the spot where MacArthur made his momentous landing fifty years before.

The landing was the real beginning.

The invasion, even if it saved Korea, was another in an endless string of invasions that explained Koreans' wariness of foreigners. That hesitance, along with a *chaebol* system that made CEOs as powerful as feds, contributed to the financial crisis of 1997. The International Monetary Fund (IMF) bailed Korea out to the tune of $35 billion, but they had conditions for the loan. Open up, create a tax haven, bring in a little foreign direct investment (FDI). Take advantage of your location, for crying out loud. A three-hour plane ride from 35 percent of the world's population.

Korea paid off the debt, but how could they expand? FEZs had once been suggested by a beloved prime minister—but where to put them? The country was 70 percent mountains. Willy Ley, founder of the German Rocket Society, once suggested that certain offshore areas—the west coast of Korea, for example—were so shallow it was tempting to think of reclaiming them, making more land, though it would be "fantastically expensive." Undeterred, Korea did King Utopus one better. Reclamation projects began in mudflats near Incheon. Engineers linked two preexisting islands for a $3 billion airport. One bridge would head directly to the mainland, and another would swoop around to the largest of the reclaimed FEZs. Inside the FEZ would be the IBD. New Songdo.

The idea to build a city from scratch emerged from the consciousness of Korea itself.

95

But who would build it? Korea didn't have real estate developers—just the *chaebol*. And anyway, if Koreans designed it, it would look Korean, which was to say, modern Korean: gargantuan apartment buildings like the mono-use monstrosities that ringed Seoul. In 1953, the country was rubble; it put itself back together in thirty years. Fast and cheap was all they knew, and that wasn't going to attract your FDI. What they needed was a joint venture with a U.S. firm calling the shots. But when the government tried to find someone to partner up, none of the *chaebol* were interested. Who wanted to be junior partner in something so far-fetched?

Posco, the Korean steel conglomerate, was split camp, at least. The construction group saw a chance for a ton of work, while the steel guys anticipated shame. But with the government twisting their arm, how could they wind up embarrassed? Get the job, earn a favor. Win-win.

In 2000, they hired a consultant out of southern California, Dr. Jay Kim.

Kim concentrated on the west coast at first, but couldn't get past second-tier marketing people. He went to ten or fifteen firms. The reply was, A, that's never been done before; B, it's never been done in Korea; C, are you kidding?; and D, U.S. real estate is booming. By March, Kim was desperate. He turned to what even then was the favored research tool of lazy under-graduates and lonely singles.

The Internet unearthed State Street Financial Center in Boston, then the largest building under construction in the world. The deal had been put together by John Hynes of Gale International. It was his first major building, but Hynes cut an interesting figure: captain of the hockey team at Harvard, drafted by the Colorado Rockies. Hurt his knee. He was the grandson of a Boston mayor who had set out to redesign Bos-ton during his tenure, so maybe the younger Hynes had the city thing in his blood.

Kim knew one guy in Boston, Tommy O'Neill—Tip O'Neill's boy. Kim called him up. Tommy said, sure, he knew John Hynes.

Hynes was putting the finishing touches on State Street when his phone rang.

"John, this is Tommy. How you doing?"

"Good."

"Uh, listen. I've got a guy on the other line, I want to patch him in. He's representing a large Korean corporation. They're interested in talking to you about a project."

"I'm negotiating the lease for State Street right now. Thanks, anyway."

"No, no, no. This is a big deal. A project in Korea. You gotta talk to him."

Kim came on the line.

"I want you to think big," he said.

"I got a pretty big tower here," Hynes said. "That's about as big as it gets."

"No. This is a master-planned city. Sponsored by the government of Korea."

"Uh, okay."

"I'd like to come in and talk to you about it."

The timing was bad, but Hynes had to admit he was interested. He and his boss, Stan Gale, both had ambitions to work on bigger projects. Hynes set an hour aside; Kim flew to Boston. He showed up with aerials and photographs and a cartoon that some government design official had produced showing what they thought the skyline of the finished city might look like: the Eiffel Tower, the World Trade Center, the Empire State Building, the TransAmerica Tower. Kim stayed three hours, talking, pleading. When Hynes admitted he was interested, Kim wanted to take him to Korea that instant. But the lease negotiation was ongoing. Hynes offered to write a letter of interest instead, on the condition that Kim not show it to Morgan Stanley, State Teachers of Ohio, or Stan Gale. They'd have his head.

"But you'll come?"

"I'll come to Korea. After the lease is signed. And after I get a passport."

96

Hynes had never left the country before he went to Korea that first time, but he'd done it often since then. I met him at Gale's offices at Fifty-seventh and Fifth in Manhattan. The offices had a view of Central Park—a view, actually, of the Frick Collection a dozen blocks north, where Holbein's painting of More hangs beside a doorway. I visited the collection the morning I met Hynes. The painting was an odd choice for Frick, who seemed to prefer portraits of doe-eyed children executed with a flattering blur. By contrast, the audio docent noted, the photorealistic detail of the stubble on More's cheek could make one's knees go weak. This appeared lost on Frick, who had hung one of the most famous portraits in the world beside a door that partially obscured it.

On the way to Gale International, I stumbled across the Utopia Café on Fifty-sixth Street. There was only half a Utopian Turkey Sandwich left in the cooler, but the guy behind the counter agreed to make me a whole one. Turkey, avocado, tomato, herb mayonnaise, roasted peppers, grilled onions, watercress.

"Do you know why it's called the Utopian Turkey Sandwich?"

"Because—" He paused; it was difficult. "I don't know why."

There were at least seven businesses in Manhattan with Utopia in their names. The café, a donut joint, a children's center, a health care agency, a jewelry story, and two escort services.

97

Hynes laced his fingers behind his head. He was a man who crossed his legs at the ankle, never the knee. He spoke in a kind of verbal bullet-point presentation and had a natural inclination to reduce narrative to summarized dialogue reclaimed from the depths of his memory. Now he waxed vaguely poetic, an average guy belly up to the bar, using a beer to crack the tap of his emotions.

"There isn't a real estate guy out there anywhere, who really enjoys his business, that wouldn't embrace this possibility. Here's a clean slate—you get to design a whole city. You get to put the pieces of the puzzle together. In fact, you get to design the puzzle. By the same token, you could spend a lifetime playing with something like that. And you'd be living in the woods in a log cabin, pumping your water."

Now it was seven years in. No one was pumping water. New Songdo was going up. The first residences, First World, a complex of four skyscrapers and eight low-rise buildings, would be occupied in a few months. It was a tenth of what the city would eventually hold. Demand was not a problem. They received sixty-five thousand applications for the first twenty-six hundred apartments: $1 billion worth of real estate sold in a day.

"You're going to see it, right?" Hynes asked me.

"This Saturday," said Mary Lou, the publicist who had arranged my trip.

"I'm right behind you. I'm leaving at midnight."

"You're leaving at two o'clock," Mary Lou told me.

"You're on the afternoon flight?" Hynes said.

"Yeah."

"You get there Sunday night. You get there at seven o'clock."

"You know all the scenarios, I can tell."

"This is trip number seventy for me. Seven, oh. Seven *hundred* trips to New York, but seventy to Korea."

98

I asked what the first phone call about Songdo to Stan Gale had been like.

"Well, what is it?" Gale had said.

Hynes tried to explain. "Stan, they want us to come in and oversee the whole thing, offices, residences, everything you can think of. Hire architects, engineers, entice FDI, Morgan Stanley, Paine Webber. They want us to create a city. They *want* a U.S. company. Why not take a look? Doesn't hurt."

"Yeah," Gale said, "let's go."

"Exactly. It's just a couple days. The lease is signed. Let's go take a look."

"Fine."

But Gale canceled at the last minute, told Hynes to go on ahead and call him if it was any good. The Koreans rolled out the red carpet. The vice mayor of Incheon showed up; there was a helicopter tour. At that point the reclamation for the New Songdo city IBD portion of the FEZ was only about one-tenth complete. In other words, the site was water. They gave him the pitch. Hub city for Northeast Asia, untapped markets, and so on. You could research the data to death, Hynes realized, but there was no greater incentive than the fact that Korea had already invested $10 billion in infrastructure. They couldn't let it fail.

That was the due diligence.

He called Gale. "Stan, get your ass over here. You got to see this, it's unbelievable. These guys are serious."

"Alright, I told you I'd be there."

Gale had been born nine days before MacArthur's Incheon

landing, and his link to utopian master planning, like mine, was personal. He'd earned his broker's wings on the Irvine Ranch in California, a master-planned project an hour or so north of Utopia Road. Gale and Hynes were a perfect fit. Hynes was Boston, urban, had a taste for the nitty-gritty of design and wanted to do towers. Gale was New York and Jersey, had the finance background, the residential experience, and was more focused on the vision thing. Yet they were the same type of non-buttoned-down guy. Gale had nurtured athletic hopes, too. Tried out for the New York Cosmos—European footballers were too tough—then took to the family business. He was third-generation real estate. When he wanted to expand north, Hynes, introduced to Gale as "Mr. Boston," was the obvious choice. Gale hired in his own image.

Now they had the chance to become the first-ever foreign owners of Korean soil.

The Koreans gave Gale the same treatment: meetings, helicopter, sketches. Hynes and Gale were salesmen finding themselves sold. China was Communist, Japan was impregnably expensive, and here was Korea, an affordable democracy right in the middle of the world's largest emerging market.

On the way home they had some fun in the airplane, tearing out pictures from travel magazines and brainstorming how the city would work. They put their puzzle together. Back in New York, they noodled on it for a while, then signed a memorandum of understanding (MOU) giving them six months to submit a plan. On September 10, 2001, Hynes met with one of the principals of Kohn Pedersen Fox (KPF), the architectural firm that eventually came onboard. The following morning slowed

things down—but only by a few months. In March 2002, repre-
sentatives of Posco, the city of Incheon, Gale, and KPF gathered at the Waldorf for the unveiling of the master plan. There
were details to work out—they needed to change a few Korean
zoning laws, no big deal—but New Songdo was on the drawing
board.

99

Another interviewer was waiting for Hynes. I had one more
question.

In addition to skyscrapers, the Koreans wanted complete
technological integration, a fully wired world. Korea and Japan both had borrowed the word "ubiquitous" to describe this.
The word had lost its meaning in adoption, and one of the central selling points of New Songdo city was that its sixty-five
thousand inhabitants, and the three hundred thousand who
would work there, would be able to avail themselves of a ubiquitous lifestyle, U-Life, a networked future where every convenience was possible. Gale International planned to stay on
when the city was finished to operate U-Life.

I wanted to know how it would work.

Hynes described it as a kind of municipal concierge service.
But it was still in formation, and not much could be stated un-
equivocally. In fact, they had just signed another MOU with
Microsoft related to U-Life. The new word for U-Life was
MAGIC. Microsoft and Gale . . . in Communication? Hynes
wasn't sure what it stood for, and he had to wait until someone
who knew more about it walked past the open door.

"Tom, what's U-Life called now? MAGIC?"

"Well, U-Life remains U-Life. MAGIC is the alliance. Microsoft and Gale . . . Microsoft and Gale . . . in Concert."

100

One evening in 1896, a wealthy businessman known as Mr. X was quietly enjoying his after-dinner cigar in the lobby of Chicago's Grand Pacific Hotel when he happened to over-hear a discussion of the "labor question." Mr. X's neighbors were indiscreet conversationalists—one could not help but eavesdrop—and as a businessman Mr. X was curious, albeit unsympathetic. It turned out that the men were headed that evening to a series of lectures on the subject, so when they rose to depart, Mr. X followed. The meeting was predictably dull, but the final speaker was a man Mr. X recognized as an old school chum. This man spoke on behalf of something called the United Corporation, which was to be a "King of Monopolies." As might be suspected, given the makeup of the audience, the talk was not well received—there were hisses and such—and the speaker ended with a rushed recommendation of a volume entitled *The Human Drift*.

Mr. X was moved despite the talk's poor reception. "I almost forgot where I was," he later recalled. "My mind had grasped the idea, and was conjuring with pictures and mathematics in a way that brought the whole scheme of the United Corporation before me like a panorama."

He rushed to a newstand and read through *The Human Drift*. Beyond the "King of Monopolies," the book proposed the creation of a fabulous city, Metropolis, which would be "a perpetual World's Fair," home to sixty million people—the bulk of the nation's population.

Mr. X was quickly convinced that Metropolis was both a sound business proposition and a profound societal advance. He committed $80 million to the project and was soon giving interviews—like that printed in the *New York Standard* on August 2, 1896—offering the argument that Metropolis was no idle speculation but foregone conclusion.

101

Except Mr. X wasn't real. Neither was the interview. In fact, both were part of *The Human Drift* (1894), which was real, a logical conundrum that seemed not to concern its author, a young hardware and bottle-stopper salesman who had been blessed with the optimistic first name King.

Before proposing the King of Monopolies, King's entrepreneurial experience was limited to losing $19,700 on a plan to develop a carbonating machine. This failure did not stymie his ambition. *The Human Drift* promised a renewal of civilization with corporate personhood as the agent of salvation. The way to fight back against competition as organizing principle, King argued, was to beat it at its own game. The United Corporation would begin as a nationwide grocery concern, and expansion into other industries would exponentialize success. Those put out of work by the United Corporation would be engaged in the construction of a seventy-mile-by-thirty-mile urban space that started at Niagara Falls and extended east

into New York State. Metropolis would be a field of gargantuan apartment buildings: twenty-four thousand of them.

Once inhabited, a variety of utopian advances would manifest. The elimination of crime and money would make law and banking obsolete. Labor would be distributed equally; everyone would retire by forty; women would finally be free. *The Human Drift* included schematics, drawings, poems, imaginary interviews, maps, and a certificate that could be clipped and used for the purchase of company shares—one dollar each.

"My friends," King wrote, "this is not politics; it is not religion. It is hard pan business sense."

That others were left unconvinced of the hardness of King's pan is evidenced by the fact that, less than a year after *The Human Drift* was published, King sought audience with William Painter, inventor of the bottle cap. Not surprisingly, Painter's advice was that King think up something bottle cap—like—disposable and designed

to generate repeat customers. A short time later, King was having his morning shave, and, on taking careful note of his blade, he experienced a vision not unlike Mr. X's grandiloquent reverie on first hearing of the United Corporation:

> In that moment it seemed as though I could see the way the blade could be held in a holder; then came the idea of sharpening the two opposite edges of the thin piece of steel that was uniform in thickness throughout, thus doubling its service.... All this came more in pictures than in thought as though the razor were already a finished thing and held before my eyes. I stood there before that mirror in a trance of joy at what I saw.

He rushed off to give his wife the news: Their fortune was made. He was right, but it was another eight years before anyone invested in King Camp Gillette's "safety razor." The Gillette Corporation would use its founder's image to promote their product, and King Gillette soon had one of the most recognizable faces in the world. It was printed more than ninety-six billion times.

102

Hynes was correct to say that you could waste a lot of time designing a model city—Gillette went on to do just that, a utopian career that combined Carlo Petrini's corporate success with Knut Kloster Jr.'s endearing fatalism. He remained active in his company for only a decade, then retired to southern California to grow dates and figs and to dabble in real estate. He never stopped tinkering on Metropolis. The United Corporation became the World Corporation, and then the People's Corporation, an evolution that earned him labels of "crack-pot" and "utopian radical socialist." The pioneer of disposable culture predicted his apartment buildings would last a thousand years. He wrote several more books fleshing out the details—a Charter, By-Laws, a Labor Bureau—and in 1910 he was granted Articles of Incorporation by the Territory of Arizona. He offered Teddy Roosevelt $1 million to become the company's first president. Roosevelt declined.

Gillette made billions selling a better chinscraper, but he couldn't unload a perfect city.

103

KPF was just a few blocks from Gale International.

James von Klemperer, lead architect on New Songdo, had two framed sets of stamps in his office. One was U.S. postage, images from the 1939 World's Fair in New York, and the other was Korean, the conceptual designs KPF had produced at the earliest stages of Songdo's development.

Von Klemperer was a smallish, mild-mannered fellow with a Harvard, Cambridge, and Princeton architectural pedigree. He claimed he hadn't been surprised when Hynes and Gale showed up with their plan. Calls like that were coming in often these days from the Middle East and Asia. The world had seen more city planning in the last twenty years than it had in the four hundred before that. Before Songdo, Von Klemperer had designed two cities himself, both for China, both unbuilt.

Hynes and Gale couldn't have imagined what they were getting themselves into when they set out to create a city on the other side of the world, Von Klemperer said. That was probably why it was coming to pass. They had innocence and energy. It had all started with a blank piece of paper. They spent some time considering cities of the past: New York, of course; Haussmann's Paris; Le Corbusier's Chandigarh. Von Klemperer knew utopian thought—in college he'd studied Saint-Simon, Fourier's phalansteries, Owen's New Harmony—and while the Songdo team was hardly made up of philosophers, he allowed that the imagination of anyone considering a city was naturally going to find its way back to optimistic musings. The trick they had to pull off was synthesizing organic process: How do you *create* that which is generally the result of serendipity? The city features they most wanted to incorporate had come about accidentally, and what they set out to implement was a kind of planned unplannedness.

An intentional city.

Songdo's central park came first, and it was a trick to convince the Koreans who had spent billions dredging the land not to build anything on it. The park meant green space—the master plan called for 34 percent—but they argued for edges. Skyscrapers on parks or water made for a towering stack of high-value property. And what would a city look like if you tried to give everyone an edge to look out on? For that they consulted the history of city planning, the circle patterns and grid patterns and star patterns that, like most of the new cities being built today, were mono-use: bedroom communities, techno cities; the Vegas fever dream of Dubai, the commerce center of Pudong; the government of Brasília; the ecosuburbs of China. Songdo was different. It was multifunction, multiuse, so it only made sense that it would draw on a variety of plans, the nuclear (Beijing), dual lobe (Shanghai), radial sectors (Vienna), and radial network (Paris), all layered together into a city of synergy. Le Corbusier's description of Rome ("the first example of Western planning on the grand scale") inspired the positioning of Songdo's more important buildings: the museum, the hospital, the trade center, and so on. That was how they got to work, with something almost like a school exercise. Small teams each took a building and produced a plausible design, and then they played a kind of street chess with the models, shifting them around on a map the size of a couple of couches, placing the structures and backing off to consider everything from the zoning envelope, to street atmosphere, to, eventually, a third dimension of the master plan: a pitched imaginary ceiling with buildings tall at the center and falling away toward the Yellow Sea.

104

Early on Songdo's marketing strategy had emphasized corporate enterprise—it would be a place to turn a buck. The Korean population, suffering from decades of architectural malnourishment, needed no incentive. They were ready for utopia. But business—the FDI—was cool at first. In 2006, well after Songdo had broken ground on a sixty-five-story trade tower, the international school, a convention center, and First

World, they announced they were looking for ways to improve New Songdo.

The city willed itself forward by becoming even more utopian.

Von Klemperer cited an upswing in ecological conscience among architects, and for developers sustainability issues, despite the added premium, had simply become something the consumer wanted. Because it was being built from the ground up, Songdo offered unique possibility. Not only would it adhere to modern environmental standards, they decided, it would become a bellwether of urban sustainability. Its Venetian canal street, populated with fish, turtles, and crustaceans, would run on wind turbine power and supply water to city cooling systems. A rainwater collection system would irrigate landscaping designed to appeal to indigenous and migratory birds. A pneumatic waste-collection system would transport all solid waste for compression and dehydration, and energy recaptured from incineration would be returned to the grid. A ten-acre Ecotarium on the central park would feature more than three hundred animal species, populating advanced educational exhibits simulating everything from mountain forest to deep-sea environments. A citywide gray-water system would recycle lavatory runoff for use in bio-urinals, and a black-water system would sort sewage into water that would be irradiated and used for road cleaning and solid waste that would pass into a methane reactor for additional energy recapture. Photovoltaic building facades, car shares, hydrogen-fuel buses, solar collection farms, underground storage for recyclables, controls on air-conditioning to reduce urban heat-island effect—all would be included in what Gale came to call the City of Ideas.

New Songdo was now 95 percent committed residential, 50 percent committed corporate.

105

Lewis Mumford's little-known early book *The Story of Utopias* (1922) effectively served as the rough draft for his seminal *The City in History* (1961). Four decades apart, the two books call on the same sources, utopians all: Plato, More, Andreae, Mercier, Bellamy, Engels, Fourier, Owen, Wells, Soria y Mata. Mumford didn't particularly care whether utopias were earnest or ironic—utopian novels and blueprints were as valid an avenue of inquiry as realized societies in considering the history of how people lived in close proximity. The basic structure of the city as we knew it had been established by 2000 BC, he wrote, and by 400 BC it had all gone terribly wrong, with overcrowding and rampant disease. The truth was, dystopia came first—it was civilization. A masculine impulse was to blame, the transmutation of a "hunter" into a "king" whose sole job was the construction of cities whose mono-use was the demonstration of his grandeur.

Thus the emergence of utopian literature meant to fix it. The solution was planned cities.

106

Mumford was more partial to Ebenezer Howard than he was to Le Corbusier or Frank Lloyd Wright—both of whom came to celebrate KPF's bread and butter, the skyscraper—but Von Klemperer agreed that New Songdo was an attempt to repair, in a Mumford-like way, the dystopia of Seoul. It might be tall, but Songdo returned to a *città felice* biological model: streets like spines and buildings that functioned like internal organs, lungs or brains. Or, if you preferred, the city was a single-cell organism, a contained live thing. Von Klemperer took a boy's delight in spreading a map out on his desk and indicating the ring of green space that was his amoeba's cell wall and the structures that, like mitochondria, let it breathe. Even though New Songdo was the largest private real estate venture in the world, it was still possible to conceive of it as microscopic, as the first sparked-life in a laboratory conducting experiments on how the city of the future might be built.

"To what degree was the design of Songdo affected by U-Life," I asked.

"None."

107

By the spring of 1935, wealthy Pittsburgh department store owner Edgar Kaufmann had grown tired of waiting for the plans of his vacation retreat. He had commissioned Frank Lloyd Wright to design a home conforming to a remote waterfall and pool where his family liked to sun and swim. Kaufmann's son had fallen under the famed architect's spell—he was living at Taliesin, Wright's school in Wisconsin—and Kaufman agreed the man was impressive. But now quite a bit of time had passed, too much time, and no plans were forthcoming. Kaufmann decided to show up in Wisconsin.

In characteristic fashion, Wright had put off the project completely. He did not begin until Kaufmann phoned from Milwaukee to say he was en route. Wright flew into a frenzied dash, and the design he completed before Kaufmann arrived, Fallingwater, is one of the more memorable of his surviving homes.

What's more surprising than the success of Wright's design is his treatment of Kaufmann. Kaufmann had also funded a model of Broadacre City, the master-planned urban project that

Wright made plenty of time for. He dabbled with it for most of his life. The docents at Taliesin—now a museum and a still-existing intentional community—repeat the apocryphal story of Fallingwater daily, but, unless asked, do not comment on the twelve-foot-square model of Broadacre City covering a wall in a small gallery of unrealized projects.

Wright agreed with Mumford that cities were a mess: He described them alternately as "mass murder," "vampires," and a "fibrous tumor," and he likened gridlock to crucifixion. He seconded the sentiment that planning could save the city—

and went further than that. His own "organic architecture," described in *The Living City* (1958) as "the natural architecture of the democratic spirit in this age of the machine," could provide precisely what must be built "if we desire salvation for our civilization." Organic architecture would eventually inspire a new nation, Usonia, a name Wright attributed to *Erewhon*'s Samuel Butler.

Broadacre City featured a range of advances typical of utopian thought: smart mechanization, vibrationless trains, abundant atomic power, effective schools, aerotaxis. Wright retained the skyscraper. Skyscrapers side-by-side made the city a graveyard, he admitted but, in keeping with Le Corbusier, whose *Contemporary City* was strangely indebted to Gillette, Wright believed the  lone skyscraper was an effective way to reduce the human footprint.

In 1956, two decades after hurrying his way through Fallingwater, he unveiled a model for a five-hundred-story megastructure that would "mop up what remains of urbanism and leave us free to do Broadacre City."

Mumford was unimpressed: "The ultimate reduction to absurdity of this whole theory of city development."

Nor would he have agreed with Usonia's social innovation. "The king is dead; long live the king," Wright wrote. "But now the king is his majesty—the American citizen."

In Korea, Stan Gale was known as Chairman Gale. I first saw him in the lounge on the twenty-seventh floor of the luxury wing of the monstrous Hotel Lotte in downtown Seoul. Foreign corporate heavyweights used the Lotte for Korean visits, and the lounge, with its panoramic view of a downtown backed by granite-capped stalactite hills and rank-and-file apartment buildings labeled Samsung or Hyundai, served as a gentleman's club for morning snacks and chats. I'd had my coffee, soy sausage, and sweet carrot juice from the buffet and was reading a newspaper's account of a series of ongoing protests in Seoul (thousands gathered in the streets for forty nights running, condemning U.S. beef imports and being water-cannoned for their trouble) when Gale walked in.

He was in a hurry. He grabbed a slice of melon but never ate it, and sat down with a friend, his back to the windows, talking mostly with his hands. He had the look of a guy waiting impatiently for his blackjack croupier to shuffle up and deal. He saw me glancing through Songdo material when his companion left, but I pretended not to notice him. I had an interview with him in a few hours. I left the hotel.

It was my second walk of the morning. The first jet-lagged meander had come at 4:00 A.M., and I had wandered down into the city's submerged crosswalks, its tiled underworld where the homeless gathered like a tribe of the masses anticipated by Wells, Dostoyevsky, and *Metropolis*, and then up again into the remnants of the older city that had been sat upon by skyscrapers, the backstreets and side streets crammed with dead neon and electric lanterns, Korean symbols like architectural sketches, and restaurant tanks of doomed octopi that observed with unnerving intelligence the comings and goings of their executioners. Seoul had a tart fecal smell that soaked even the best parts of the city—they had failed to heed Benjamin Ward Richardson's *Hygeia: A City of Health* (1876), which warned against "gases emanating from the water-closets"—but it wasn't because Koreans lacked industriousness. I stopped to watch a woman use a short twig broom to pry out cigarette butts from a metal grate, tidying up the area behind her street kiosk. There was little refuse in general. What the Koreans had lacked was a plan. It wasn't that they had failed to assimilate four thousand years of city development in three decades, it was that the city itself had been another invasion. It was the story of Godzilla, basically. Godzilla doesn't destroy skyscrapers. He is one. The alien mother ship of the modern world had set down gently, all Seoul went the way of Willy Loman's backyard, and Koreans assimilated their colonizers by applying the aesthetics of the cheap beach motel to the skyscraper. Capitalism and an unmatched work ethic grew the city in all directions like a predatory weed.

Back at the Lotte, the automobile valets had arrived for the day, Korean men, something sinister about them in black top hats and white gloves, using long mops to dust diplomatic vehicles clean of sand blown in from the Gobi.

The day was beginning for professionals by the time of my second walk. Young men all awkwardly in suits, clothes worn with no sense of history, chain-smoking in groups with nubs held close to their lips like children blowing soap bubbles, and young women all in tight skirts, either bare-legged or fishnetted, sashaying along in heels that proved you could exchange one kind of foot binding for another and mistake it for emancipation.

Some wore surgical masks tight on their faces against the shit smell and desert dust, others wore surgical masks loose around their ears as a fashion statement. The city was already international in that Scott Joplin and Cuban jazz hit the streets from Western-style cafés, but it was peculiar, too, with riot police already piling off buses and jogging into marching-band formations to prepare for that night's round of beef protests.

I came across an unusual storefront: Ubiquitous Dream Hall. It was some kind of museum. They didn't have a tour in English until the afternoon.

A squadron of the villainous valets blocked the elevator back at the luxury wing.

"Wait a minute," one of them told me.

"What am I waiting for?"

"President."

"Of what company."

"Paraguay."

109

When Chairman Gale first met Bill Gates, it wasn't the first time Gates had had an opportunity to join an urban initiative in a real estate setting. So far he'd shied away, because no one had offered a complete solution. New Songdo caught his attention. He committed to making it a city of the future.

"You know," Gale told him, "it's not about just the one city."

"No, I figured," Gates said.

"Six continents. Twenty cities. Connectibility."

"Right. We're with you."

Gale told stories a little like Hynes, compressing scenes to conversations, conversations to chats, thoughts to soliloquies. Gale's offices in the Seoul Financial Center didn't have quite the views of his New York office (though the waiting room had display fans of a magazine called *Ubiquitous*), and Gale seemed a little uncomfortable with public relations people and Dr. Maing, head of U-Life, seated around a conference table listening to his life story. Up close, Gale had something of the aging comedian to him, a man now too chunky and old for the slapstick raconteur he'd once been. When I told him I'd grown up in Utopia Road, he knew the place by its real name and reveried his way back to the California broker days. The experience had made him a student of master planning, but the basic interest in city planning had come even earlier.

"I guess this is where you get accused of being a visionary."

"Yeah," Gale said, "and kind of crazy, too. I've had this thing since I was a kid—I don't know what it is—to build cities. I know it sounds crazy. For a long time I couldn't actually tell people about it, because they'd have me put away, but I've had this passion since childhood. The frustration I had is that until technology came along, I didn't see how it would be possible. I knew how long it took to get *a* building up. When technology reached the real-estate industry, I started thinking: You're going to be able to do this. So we created a formula, and we created the quality of life. That's the DNA, if you will, of the city."

"Six continents," Dr. Maing interjected, "twenty cities."

Gale nodded. China and India had already asked for Songdos, he said. The Middle East had invited him over, and Eastern Europe looked good, too. So far all he'd been able to say to interested parties was, come take a look at what we have—then get in line.

"But that's our goal, our business strategy moving forward. Songdos on six continents, twenty cities of the future connected, using our same partners and the same formula we have here. This one is taking us fifteen years, start to finish. The next will come down to seven and a half. My goal is to get a city up, start to finish, in five years."

Gale admitted that he didn't know a lot about his predecessors, Ebenezer Howard, James Rouse, and so on, but he had a different model.

"The guy that was a little nutty this way, and this sounds crazy, was Peter the Great. He was a master planner. Now, I know he had slave labor, or whatever you want to call it, but look at that. Have you been to St. Petersburg? It's his baby. And it didn't take that long, considering the magnitude. So that's my guy."

110

The plan for Filarete's star-shaped city, Sforzinda, produced in Milan between 1461 and 1464, takes the form of an imagined dialogue between Filarete and Piero de' Medici, the prince for whom the imaginary city was intended as instruction in "the modes and measures of building."

Early in the fictional lessons, the Florentine architect advises his student, "There is nothing made by the hand that does not partake of drawing in one way or another."

The prince is unimpressed; he's ready to be done with art exercises, and the architect has been ignoring his plans. "Let us leave this discussion and subtlety for the present," he decrees. "Did you understand what I want done?"

"Yes, my lord."

"Is there a means by which this castle can be built quickly?"

"I think there will be a way, because we have masters and workers, stone and lime without lack. When does your lordship wish to make a beginning?"

"I want to start tomorrow morning."

"Let your lordship be there and on time, so we can begin to lay out the city and to build the principal buildings that are most necessary to a city."

While the plan for Sforzinda was admittedly spare, one might choose to forgive Filarete's architectural understatement and emphasize instead his skills as a tutor and his delicate touch with a demanding pupil. Mumford refused. He dismissed Filarete's star-shaped city as "medieval in spirit." It failed to recognize that the star-shaped city had first been proposed by Aristophanes— as a joke. Kings and architects alike had opted for a pretty design rather than a viable plan. Sforzinda was the first ideal city of the Renaissance, and its influence,

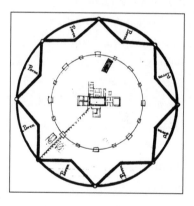

Mumford lamented, ensured that the "wild joke of Aristophanes became the characteristic mode of baroque thought."

III

A few decades after Sforzinda, a Spanish priest in Oran, serving the crown by rooting out corruption, received an intriguing offer. The occupation of New Spain was not going well. The plan to bring about a new reign of Christ by converting indigenous peoples had gone terribly wrong. Plopping one culture down on top of another had made for chaos. The first attempt to restore law and order was led by a man later likened to Himmler. There was further death and plunder. Vasco de Quiroga, a priest with a degree in canon law, was a perfect choice for the second team that was being sent to salvage the colonial adventure.

Quiroga took some time to ponder the offer. One day he happened to overhear a group of monks reciting a psalm that promised good things in return for sacrifice. It was New Spain's natives calling, he believed. He accepted.

Quiroga was born in the same year as Thomas More and, like More, was known for legal rigidity, humanist tendencies, political savvy, and occasional ruthlessness. Had More taken his interest in monasteries a bit more seriously (or had he taken his sexuality a bit *less* seriously), he might have *been* Quiroga. Quiroga had almost certainly heard of More before he went to New Spain—the empire was in the grip of an Erasmus fascination—but when he met Mexico's first bishop, Juan de Zumárraga, Quiroga was introduced formally. Zumárraga gave him a copy of *Utopia*.

As *Utopia* was set in the New World, it can perhaps be forgiven that Quiroga remained deaf to its satire. He claimed he was "inspired by the Holy Spirit" when he read the book. He devised a plan to create cities for the natives based on More. Quiroga was hardly the only Spaniard to attempt city planning in the New World—starting with the fortress Columbus built from the wrecked timbers of the *Santa Maria*, the Spanish built five hundred cities—but he was the only master planner to hear God's voice in More's thin treatise. He saw *Utopia*, as one biographer put it, as "the only possible cure for a tragic situation."

In his first visit to Michoacán, where in a few years he would become bishop, he appointed local town officials and registered twenty-five citizens for a village to be called Granada. The town's application was dismissed as "poorly planned." Writing to higher authorities in Spain, Quiroga called for *Utopia*-scale cities of six thousand families. He extolled More's virtues ("ingenious man, more than human") and suggested ordinances also drawn from *Utopia*. The letter went ignored.

Quiroga refused to give up. He crafted another proposal that borrowed from More's and Erasmus's translation of the *Saturnalia*. Quiroga proved impervious to the humor of Lucian as well. The New Spain natives were unfinished people, he wrote, but they were also closer to their golden age. By contrast, Europe had already become a world filled with "iron and steel and worse." *Utopia* offered the opportunity of elevating the natives, reshaping their behavior. Quiroga's critics called his plan an attempt to create "a new kind of human being."

Two days after he sent his second proposal to Spain, More was beheaded in England.

Mumford's treatment of Wright and Filarete suggests he would have been equally dismissive of an attempt to use More as a blueprint. Notably, he wasn't. *The City in History* describes Utopia's capital, Amaroute ("city of shadows"), in great detail. Mumford got the joke of Aristophanes, but More's passed him by. Amaroute, he said, offered a possible outline for the "social city of the future."

Which is precisely what Quiroga set about creating once his second proposal was dismissed, and he ascended to the bishopric. Defying orders, he founded a number of midsized villages, equipped with hospitals, churches, and schools. The proto-democracy, using Utopian laws, left much power with the natives, and communities shared profits from local crafts that are still known today. Quiroga instituted a six-hour workday, a system of free education, and a policy of rotating responsibility for communal meals. Utopia worked. Quiroga fussed with his ordinances for the rest of his life. He lived to ninety-five. Half a century after he died, a visitor to the region noted that the remaining natives were still "imitating the monks, living together in communities and devoting themselves to prayer and the pursuit of a more perfect life."

112

Carl Seaholm, an old buddy of Stan Gale's and Dr. Maing's American counterpart in U-Life, tried to explain the U-Life concept to me.

"So it's sort of a virtual butler?"

"Yeah, but easier."

Seaholm didn't know where the ubiquitous idea came from, but it made a good story for FDI, he said, and for making cities in general. U-Life was effortless access to goods, services, information technology, and entertainment. What you wanted in a technological city of the future, he said, was a "distributed management ecosystem."

"We've got big dreams. If we do this wrong, we'll only do it once."

"Are you the only buddy of Stan's from way back?"

"Oh, no. Stan's a big believer in relationships. In doing something like this, it's enormously important that you have a few folks around that you can trust."

113

Sal wakes when her alarm clock asks, "Coffee?"

"Yes," she mumbles.

Her window filters the day's first light and displays current tracking information on her children. The kitchen has prepared breakfast, and she uses an electronic pen to highlight a line in a newspaper. The paper e-mails the quote to her office. On her way to work, her foreview mirror advises an alternate route to avoid traffic and guides her to a parking spot. The telltale by her door is from Joe, her virtual office mate. He wants to discuss a document on the liveboard. The text appears on the wall.

"I've been wrestling with this paragraph all morning," Joe's voice says.

Sal sits back, reads, stops. She uses a stylus to circle a word that bugs her.

"I think it's this term *ubiquitous*. It's just not in common enough use, and makes the whole thing sound a little formal. Can we rephrase?"

Ubiquitous computing was first proposed in 1988 by a computer scientist at Xerox's Palo Alto Research Center. Mark Weiser played drums in a band called Severe Tire Damage, later became a professor in Maryland, and died in 1999 of stomach cancer.

He had proposed four basic computing principles:

1. The purpose of a computer is to help you do something else.
2. The best computer is a quiet invisible servant.
3. The more you can do by intuition, the smarter you are; the computer should extend your *unconscious*.
4. Technology should create calm.

In 1996, Weiser created Sal and Joe—phantoms like Gillette's Mr. X or Wright's Usonian citizen—to serve as fictional salesmen of utopia. Sal and Joe were inhabitants of the "third wave" in computing that would follow the ages of mainframes and personal computers. Ubiquity would be the age of calm technology.

The term barely dented the United States, but after Weiser died it became an anthem in Japan and Korea. In 2001, both countries went high-tech with vowels. "E" for electronic, "I" for information. Just two years later they transitioned to "U." In 2003, ubiquitous, meaning "anywhere, anytime communications," saturated a white paper from Korea's Ministry of Information and Communication. The goal was a "ubiquitous world."

One scholar characterized the transition as "u-topia into **u-life.**"

114

I went to the Ubiquitous Dream Hall in Seoul. I tagged along with a large Indian family that had arranged their own tour. It was a live version of what Weiser had done with fictional characters, a guided excursion through a typical day in a ubiquitous world, a trip from home, to commute, to office, and home again, attended by a docent who spoke lovingly of "warm ubiquitous life." The home had retinal scan keys, a remote-control drop box for groceries, a refrigerator that arranged deliveries when the milk soured, a service robot, automatic lighting and blinds, and an automated vacuum cleaner that set to work just as we stepped into the next exhibit. The bus stop gave us arrival times and offered advice on alternate routes, and we could network with our home computer from the monorail that took us to work. The office featured 3D visual conferencing and targeted speakers that made translation nonintrusive. At lunch, touch-screen tabletops eliminated waitstaff and placed all the newspapers of the world beside our menus. On the way home we walked past the "ubiquitous tree," which made cricket noises when we neared and flickered tiny lightbulbs.

"Since we can't see fireflies in the cities anymore," the docent concluded, "we made this tree."

I toured a palace, found an ancient teahouse like a terrarium, with philodendrons and parrots and slow lute music, and walked down to the Cheonggyecheon River, Seoul's only significant green space. The Cheonggyecheon had been the city's waterfront for six hundred years. It was also its sewer. The river was buried in 1978, replaced with a highway, and in recent years it had been excavated again by Seoul's mayor, who went on to become Korea's president just in time to make the bad beef deal with George W. Bush. The Cheonggyecheon was below street level, a cement-walled canal with artificial rocks and light landscaping. It was barely green.

I walked until the night's beef protests began. People carried candles in plastic cups and held signs against their chests. They gathered at the foot of skyscrapers to sing songs with Soviet melodies and Korean lyrics. A couple of stories up, diners in lighted windows pointed down at the droves lying prostrate in the street. The protest was not over *whether* to import U.S. beef but over the *age* of the beef, which determined its susceptibility to disease.

The United States did not test the entire cow for bovine spongiform encephalopathy because Americans ate only the muscle.

Koreans ate the whole cow.

115

Gillette: "The machinery in these buildings will also be made as nearly automatic as possible, not only in itself, but, where practical, from one machine to another."

Wright: "Are we ever to survive the ubiquitous machine?"

116

I ran into Gale in the club lounge on the morning I was to receive a tour of the Songdo site. He was there early with three or four people who worked for him, and when he saw me, he called out, "Ah, here's our writer! Come join us!"

The others excused themselves; Gale and I moved to some couches. He dismissed the beef protesters. "You get out there, you sing songs, you light a candle—it's fun!" He steered our conversation to a story of himself as a boy, looking down from airplanes and seeing cities from above and realizing they had been planned. Cities were his fate, but he wasn't overconfident. He could see the dangers of planning, too. He could see that Songdo and U-Life might tweak the dystopian fears of Westerners nursed on individuality and privacy and materialism.

"It will either be a very cool place," he said of Songdo, "or it will be a very lonely place."

Which surprised me a little. Truth be told, Gale was not a man I would agree with about many things, but I couldn't bring myself to dislike him. Maybe it was the innocence and the energy. Or maybe it was something else. If utopia really was the only way to battle back against dystopia, if the world truly needed the occasional utopian nudge, then what should one make of the fact that the history of utopian thought proves that earnest utopians, on their own, can neither build nor buy their visions? If a fictional utopia required fictional salesmen, then shouldn't a real utopia need a real salesman? I wasn't particularly drawn to Gale, but you don't have to like the guy who sells you your house to like your house. Now he was trying to sell me on the idea that Songdo's vision was his own. But that part of it was bunk. Songdo came from Korea, it came from Jay Kim, and it came from Von Klemperer, and its most clearly utopian features were included not because Gale believed in them, but because the world for which Songdo was intended was becoming, at least in terms of ecology and sustainability, a bit utopian itself. In other words, the idea for Songdo, like its design, was organic, the product of a plurality of imaginations. But still, it needed an agent. It seemed entirely possible that Gale, entirely by accident, had wound up with the right set of skills to fix the world's troubles. Utopia Road had been another real estate agent's attempt at humor, but Gale wasn't kidding, and did it matter that he hoped to marry profit and perfection? You could criticize Songdo's master plan for failing to include low-income housing, but would you really be utopian if you thought you'd need it? That Songdo just might work had attracted champions of broad political stripes. Former Peace Corps official and Democratic presidential envoy Richard Holbrooke once told a Korean audience, "You have repeatedly defied predictions and overcome obstacles that would have defeated lesser people. I know that, at Songdo City and elsewhere, you will do it again." And former Republican New Jersey governor and Environmental Protection Agency director Christine Todd Whitman described Songdo as a project that could "reclaim the balance between human activity and environmental vitality that is so essential to our global future."

Whitman, Gale said at breakfast, had agreed to join his board of directors on the condition that he follow through with Songdo's green imperative.

"Does it ever feel," I asked, "like you're a bit of a king?"

"It does. But it's not social engineering. The buildings—the hardware—that's easy. We're worried about the software."

117

Ten thousand construction workers crammed the Songdo site, Korean men and women, all dressed in Posco overalls slightly too large for them, hunching over screaming cement saws or welding wands with their tongues of blue heat or grunting in groups to heft huge panes of glass that would be the city's most recognizable feature. Songdo boasted progressive construction practices—recycling metal, acoustical tile, and gypsum wallboard would reduce landfill disposal by 75 percent—but it didn't prevent the construction site from looking a little apocalyptic, as though it was not a city going up but one coming down. The four skyscrapers of First World jutted Kilimanjaro-like out of nothingness. Cranes studded the island like a vast herd of brontosaurus trapped in a lake of tar. Ground level was wasteland. There were roads and weeds—the city's landscaping was taking root at a remote nursery—and swells of clayish soil that made the bioswales of the central park. On every fence there was a banner that read: Posco: You Dream It, We Build It.

It was a line from a Stan Gale speech.

In charge of it all was a man named Moore. David Moore was a quiet Brit who had been working in Korea before Songdo began, and he claimed never to have thought, not even for a moment, that his job made him pharaoh's foreman. Moore took me through the convention center first. One of the only times I heard him speak was to call an actual foreman's attention to a world map on the convention center wall. The map marked the location of important cities. Moore indicated Korea.

"This needs to be changed. It should say Songdo. Not Seoul. Songdo."

The Korean foreman smiled and nodded.

The elevators in First World had only recently started working, and we rode up to the thirty-sixth floor, to a finished model of one of the apartments—a mock-up for those who had been making payments for years now already. We slipped off our shoes to tread gently on the dark hardwood floors and looked out the broad windows on the edge the building viewed by design. It looked over the central park. Down below was the muddy trench that would be Songdo's subway line, and in the distance was the bald, still muddy golf course designed by Jack Nicklaus. The trade tower was only half complete, but we could see all of it, like a towering ant colony. The apartment's appliances looked to the future; its woodwork looked to the past. There was enough space for the two- and three-generation families that were Korean tradition.

Moore took me through the central park, the nearly completed school. An entire branch campus of Incheon University was rising in the near distance, but it wasn't Moore's jurisdiction, so he only pointed. We ate a quiet lunch at a restaurant called Paradise. Moore was the only Songdo representative I met who actually planned to live in the city when it was done.

Back in Seoul, I took a quick dinner at the club lounge. The next table was filled with Gale people.

"People travel so much these days. They see these wonderful new buildings and they want these things for themselves. People are saying, you can't do this, no one will buy it. But they are—they're buying it. The average person sees the politics, but they need to see the plan. People want to be where the action is, right? So what's the incentive for companies? That's the challenge. So build the bridge, and they'll come. You can't prove it, but if you build it, they'll come."

118

I skimmed the edge of the beef protests again that night, then cut away into a labyrinthine *dong*—a district or neighborhood—to find good Korean beer served in ceramic mugs. The neon tunnels, the spastic whizzing barber poles, and the light bars of police vehicles were doubled in puddles of the day's rain. Gangs of businessmen, done with their white-collar days, stumbled the wet streets looking for trouble; pairs of girls, arm in arm, brushed trouble by; and young men, smoking, loitering, spike-haired, *were* the trouble. I paused outside Western Amigo Bar and Two Two Fried Chicken but stopped finally at a place without a name. Then I returned to a subterranean faux English pub beneath the Lotte. I sat at the bar. A Korean lounge singer did a sexy jog in place in time to a horrid repertoire.

"Hey, how are you?"

"Good! You?"

"Good! It's been a good day."

It was Seaholm, Gale's pal, coming back from the john. He invited me to join Gale and a few others in a back room, there to celebrate a successful meeting with another corporate bigwig.

"It all came together," Seaholm said. "We didn't have to jump through any hoops today!"

In back, Gale was letting his jib to the wind. He was telling a joke about an Arab sheikh who had ordered eight Black Hawk helicopters for recreational purposes. The punch line was, "Then he ordered forty more!" The table laughed: Dr. Maing, Seaholm, a Korean girl beside Gale whose name was Sasha, and two younger executives named Kyle and Brian, both related to Gale. When I took out my notebook, someone said, "Are you working?"

Before I replied, Gale burst out, "He's always working!" He ordered another round for the table.

I took out a facsimile of Gillette's *The Human Drift* and showed Gale the apartment buildings the razor mogul had pre-scribed. Gale pincered his way through the book, looking for pictures.

"Twenty-four thousand of these? Geez—could use a little architecture. Damn, I thought we were first!"

The table laughed again, but Gillette triggered a debate. It was clear that Metropolis's endless rows would have made only Gillette happy, but was there a good way to describe what a city, a plan, needed to provide?

"Fulfillment," Gale said. "Something."

His nephew spied an opportunity. "Stan makes a great point. Quality of life? It's a joke! Well, it's not a joke—but we throw it around like a business term. 'Enjoyment' is big pic-ture."

This quieted us. Sasha's tired eyes pinned Gale—her signal that the night should end. Gale reached for her hand and took just a moment longer.

"People are inspired by ideas just a little bit bigger than they can imagine for themselves. Five years, we can do. The buildings only take three. Two more for all the bullshit. City of Ideas! I know how it sounds—Michelangelo, crazy, whatever. But, City of Ideas!"

A GUN

103. All the [citizens] are soldiers; they are
all exercised in the use of arms.
—THOMAS SPENCE,
The Constitution of a Perfect Commonwealth
(1798)

I am verily of the opinion that Fantastick
Eutopian Common Wealths (which some
witty men, some Philosophers, have drawn
unto us) introduced among men, would
prove far more loathsom and be more
fruitful of bad consequences than any of
those of the Basest allay yet known.
—*A Serios Aviso to the Good People of this*
Nation, Concerning that Sort of Men,
called Levellers (1649)

119

So do all these utopians, these sometimes charming visionaries driven to good work by their hearts or their wallets, mean utopia has escaped its tendency to lurch toward its opposite? The truth is, utopias don't always slip, and any sympathetic survey of utopian thought, after acknowledging itself as utopian, must allow that the slouch toward tyranny of some utopias is not a misunderstood joke but part of the plan.

120

One of the more curious features of *Utopia*—and a major plot point in the academic battle over how to unriddle the book—is the Utopians' approach to war. They claim to despise war, but actually they're pretty good at it. Utopian life requires regular military training for men and women both, and Hythloday notes that "their skill in the arts of war gives them confidence." Which is not to say they go to war with relish—they don't. They prefer to employ mercenaries to do their dirty work, and to this end a number of savage nations are conveniently close at hand. One local tribe of fearsome warriors, the Zapoletes, lack the Utopians' enlightened views on property and money and are easy to hire into service for missions they are not likely to survive.

As warriors themselves, the Utopians abandon chivalry.

The first thing they do when engaging an enemy prince is attempt to bribe the opposing populace into assassinating him. Next, a kind of Utopian Special Forces unit sneaks behind enemy lines to target generals. They do all this knowing full well that other nations find it dishonorable. They don't care; they value victory by cunning more than victory by bloodshed. The Utopians are not without mercy—once they have conquered a city, they don't harm civilians. They put to death only spies and any who oppose surrender.

Commentators on *Utopia* worry over how to make sense of all this. The vision looks a bit too much like Mao's China, some argue, and what should one make of the fact that More's feast was celebrated in the calendar of the Red Army? There were really two sets of utopians who un-got the joke of More. The first were those who took *Utopia* as a blueprint while ignoring the fact that its perfect world was not particularly peaceful. The second— less routinely acknowledged, but all in all a more substantial body of the witless—assumed violence was essential to any programmatic new world order.

Kidding or no, F. T. Marinetti wasn't the first to suggest you'd have to machine-gun your way to the promised land.

121

Edward Bulwer-Lytton—whose most famous published words are "It was a dark and stormy night"—perhaps deserves more credit than he has received for helping to make a dark and stormy night of most of the twentieth century. His utopian novel *The Coming Race* (1871) offered nothing new by way of its plot but sounded a clarion call with its particular pattern of tropes. *The Coming Race* is one of a fleet of novels to position paradise underground—*Symzonia* (1820), *Journey to the Center of the Earth* (1864), *Etidorpha* (1895), etc.—and its emphasis on a newly discovered power is consistent with the suggestions of many other utopians who caught a glint of the industrial revolution just as it appeared on the horizon.

But Bulwer-Lytton's new power source wasn't just a prescient anticipation of mechanized factories or kitchen appliances. The force of *The Coming Race*—Vril (read: virile)—is a kind of hypertelepathy harnessed by those underground utopians, the Vril-ya. In the book's backstory, the ancestors of the Vril-ya (of solid Aryan stock) discovered within themselves an all-permeating bodily fluid that could be channeled for use in the same way certain undersea animals generate electricity. The power was used for good and healing at first, though its potential as a weapon became apparent soon enough. Conflict erupted, a war that did not end until the only ones left were those who had "brought the art of destruction to such perfection as to annul all superiority in numbers, discipline, and military skill." In other words, Bulwer-Lytton's perfect world was made possible by an early incarnation of the philosophy of mutual assured destruction. The Vril-ya put all their actual weapons in mothballs and concluded that human perfection, either genetic or social, was impossible without an incendiary baptism. They became a peaceful people with all the powers of *Star Wars* Jedi knights.

Which was a lure too sumptuous not to chomp down on. Vril crept into the real world. A Vril-ya club formed in London around the turn of the century, and texts appeared claiming Bulwer-Lytton had modeled his power on ancient writings based in fact. An early exercise in fan fiction saw Vril incorporated into a novel in which a race of people called the "aerians" used the force to establish world dominion through the exercise of air power.* And during the Boer War, a "fluid beef" product called Bovril was used as military provision. Kipling was said to have a tooth for Bovril's "liquid life."

In Germany, *The Coming Race* played a role in the blending of race doctrine, mythology, and theosophy. Members of a new Vril society—dedicated to the awakening of the Aryan race—openly hoped to cultivate a power that would enable empire. The Nazis sent expeditions to Antarctica to explore caves that might be gateways to the Vril-ya and experimented with a saucer-shaped aircraft called the Vril Machine.

122

All of which is spooky and peculiar and maybe apocryphal. But what about actual guns?

In 1890, Viennese economist and social Darwinist Theodor Hertzka produced a utopian novel, *Freeland*, that appeared to reply directly to Bulwer-Lytton. Hertzka insisted that the fictional pioneers who founded his ideal country did so without the help of "supernatural properties and virtues." They were just well-armed men.

Freeland is utopia as white man's burden: A hearty band of safari types set off for the subcontinent, announce their arrival in country with cannon volleys, expedition their way to a

---

* The twentieth century's string of novels describing racially pure Edens brought about by holocaust is fully documented in Sven Lindqvist's *A History of Bombing*.

region they dub Eden Vale, and establish their local reputation with a war whose duration is mercifully short, thanks to their deadly aim. It takes Freeland just twenty years to establish itself as a global superpower, not to mention civilize its neighbors by arming them strategically. The Freelanders achieve all this not with a standing army but with a populacewide initiative toward military training: All their lads are exposed to "profound ballistic studies," and soon two hundred thousand of them are enough to repel any invading army. By the end of the book they hardly ever war; they just train for it.

"It is only this very superiority in bodily exercises," a visitor is told, "which secures to us Freelanders the inviolable peace which we enjoy."

123

Like *Looking Backward*, *Freeland* inspired a number of societies dedicated to bringing its vision to pass. They flowered and wilted. So whence the practical application? Who—like Engels transmuting utopia into science—applied the theory that peace could be achieved through superior firepower?

Surprisingly, the basic idea survived World War I; not surprisingly, a German writer helped keep it alive for the sequel.

When Ernst Jünger wasn't indulging his second great love— entomology—he set himself the task of repairing the German ego after its first great blow of the twentieth century. An officer in the trenches—the youngest ever recipient of the Pour le Mérite—he wrote a memoir of his early battle experiences, *Storm of Steel* (1920), in which he recast the initial defeat of the Fatherland as tragic valor. Jünger wrote lyrically of British soldiers crumbling in his scope as he picked them off with a sniper's rifle and fondly of Scottish soldiers who wrote to him years after the war with descriptions of the wounds he had inflicted on them. Germany might have lost, the book claimed, but war was still the most vivid game in town, and anyway it was all in good fun. Jünger was never a Nazi (though he exchanged signed books with Hitler), and he would have admired modern Israel's martial vigor, yet a later tract, *The Worker* (1932), appears to adopt as its primary thesis a causal link between utopia and violence.

> It is obvious that a new world order, as the consequence of world dominion, results, not as a gift from heaven or as the product of a utopian reason, but from a chain of wars and civil wars. . . .

> But impressions of the heart and systems of spirit are refutable, while a thing is irrefutable—and such a thing is the machine gun. . . .

> The landscape of war . . . offers the image of high closure and efficiency accelerated by emergency. Here, the feverish cultivation of battle machines or the artificial replacement of essential raw materials—which occurs with the same haste that governed the forging of new armor for Achilles in the Vulcan workshops—reveals the extent to which the technological will might appear as a special expression of the will of a superior race.

124

Utopian novels suggesting paradise lay on the far side of conflict, and a utopian tract lauding weaponry and violence made
a promising theoretical battery. The failure of that battery to
achieve either world dominion or a superior race (excepting
perhaps Jünger himself, who died in 1998 at age 102) was the
final nail for utopia, which became, in war's aftermath, as
H. G. Wells put it in 1914, a "noun and an adjective of abuse."
The grim trajectory is clear in retrospect: Jünger, Hertzka, and
Bulwer-Lytton all harkened back to the original militarized
society that both Plato and More had taken as their model:
Sparta.

The primary model for King Utopus was practically fictional
himself. Plutarch's life of Lycurgus cites fifty previous biogra-
phers whose accounts varied widely even on basic facts. Plutarch
culled a speculative narrative. Lycurgus was descended from
Hercules. He came of age in a time when the royal power in
Sparta had lapsed. He ascended to the throne after the people
rose up and killed first his father and then his brother. Lycurgus
ruled well for eight months before it was discovered that a new-
born child was the rightful heir. He went into voluntary exile
when plots formed to kill the boy and return Lycurgus to the
throne.

He traveled: to Lacedæmon, Asia, and Egypt, acquiring
learning of statecraft and soldiery along the way. The best
world, he came to think, would combine the temperance of
the Cretins and the indulgence of the Ionians. Years passed.
Lycurgus returned to Sparta, executed a bloodless coup, and
set about implementing a concise set of new laws: a senate to

share power with the king; all land distributed equally to all people; nonnecessary arts eliminated; a new monetary system; collective child rearing; and compulsory communal evening meals. For this last, Lycurgus was mugged and had one of his eyes put out.

Still, scholars cite Sparta as that rare instance when a monarch succeeded in transforming the psychology of an entire populace. The focus of the nation turned solely to civil preparedness, the use of the skills of war to ensure self-preservation. All craft and trade professions were outlawed. The country became a permanently armed camp—Fortress Sparta, in one characterization—and the Spartans themselves became enthralled with espionage and intelligence gathering and created their own secret police force, the Crypteia. The transformation hinged on a heady masculinity. Spartans became men of few laws, and fewer words. Spartan women were emancipated, though mainly in the sense of becoming masculine themselves. Boys were initiated into adulthood with ritualized homosexual relationships with older mentors. The value of a Spartan soldier became legendary throughout the Greek world. Sparta was the only city-state to perpetuate itself without a wall protecting it. Walls were effeminate.

Sparta's fall, after five hundred years, was predicted by one of its original laws: Do not wage war against your neighbor too often; it will only make them good at it. One account of the life of Lycurgus claimed that his skills as a leader and general were so great he never had to use them. His descendants were less temperate, and later conflicts against the Thebans, whom they had once enslaved, sowed their ruin.

125

If utopia's link to violence was causal, and if the history of violent utopias traced back to one whose inauguration by the sword ensured it would perish by the same, then what should be made of the fact—as earnest, modern utopians creep along trying to sustain the dream—that a new Lycurgus, and a new Sparta, was threatening to rise in the desert of Nevada, a sling's shot from Death Valley?

I drove west from Vegas, through Red Rock Canyon and up into a small mountain range. I watched the sunrise in my rearview mirror, lost a raving radio host's signal at the pass, and coasted down onto a plain straddling the California border, a vast blank slab of Bureau of Land Management land speckled with an army of cactus. It was that blankness—not to mention amenable laws—that had made Nevada home to Front Sight Resort, the largest civilian combat training facility in the world.

My Four-Day Defensive Handgun course started at 8:00 A.M. on a Friday morning. I drove up to a chain-link gate forty-five minutes early. I was tenth in line.

126

Precisely on time a chubby man in the gray and black uniform of Front Sight's instructional staff let us in. The line of cars snaked back half a mile by then. We slithered inside, parked in formation. Additional staff waited for us at a row of tables for registration. Within minutes I was assigned a Glock 9mm handgun. A staff member cinched my belt for me and slipped two magazines into the holster he nestled gently against my thigh.

"Bullets always point at the bad guys."

My name was taped to my chest and back, and my range number scribbled on my hand in ink. In a place where everyone was wearing a gun, I was reminded, it would not be a good idea to take mine out of my holster unless I was instructed to do so.

I locked myself in a porta-potty—the brown room, in local speak—and took out my Glock anyway. It dragged my hand toward the smelly floor. The portent of a gun gives it a kind of deadweightiness, like a heavy metal that surprises you with its crazy mass-to-weight ratio. The Glock had swoopy ergonomic features, a hot rod's sexy curves. A handful of brass ammunition—they'd given me boxes of it—soaked my palm with the drippy luster of treasure. Back on my hip, the gun felt awkward, like a colostomy bag at capacity.

I wandered into the pro shop while the weekend's student body filed in and armed up. The store's entire staff was packing. Most of the merchandise was goods—speed loaders, rifle sights, camouflage—and there was exactly one film and one book for sale, each filling a couple shelves. Aaron Zelman's *Innocents Betrayed* documented the worldwide holocaust that had been perpetrated on unarmed civilians by their own governments, and the jacket copy of one-time Libertarian presidential candidate Michael Badnarik's *Good to Be King* claimed that the text inside revealed "why, in America, *you* are the king."

I followed the crowd as it began to gather in the main meeting hall, a large chamber like a semitemporary mess erected
in a war zone. The model for Front
Sight's planned gated community
stood in a corner.

In a year or two they would begin construction on the town of
Front Sight: a couple of hundred
single-family homes; some condos;
hotels; streets called Second Amendment Drive and Sense of
Duty Way; an airstrip; and a K–12 school with armed teachers,
all of it wrapping around the facility's maze of tall dirt berms,
its complex of shooting ranges and enclosures for scenario training. The main pitch line for the town of Front Sight claimed it
would be the safest community in America, because everyone
in it would be armed.

The model revealed a peculiar feature: It would be a gated
community without a gate. It had no exterior wall.

Three hundred of us had gathered for the weekend's curricu-
lum of beginning handgun courses and more elaborate training
in the rifle and the shotgun. Front Sight's operations manager
took a stage to welcome us. He asked how many of us were First
Family members. About a third raised a hand. The First Family
was a kind of advanced club that made you eligible for free
classes for the rest of your life—countrywide, there were twelve
thousand First Family members. The weekend's team of instructors lined up before us for introductions. Many of them had
been Front Sight students themselves, which meant that Front
Sight had already become a self-perpetuating combat-trained

alternative to the military. Within the past year, Front Sight had produced and distributed a television show that pitted its students against military servicemen and law enforcement personnel in shooting contests. The results proved that motivated civilians with good training outperformed the professionals. This was the training we would receive.

We were dismissed to our ranges.

127

The range master for my class of forty was a man named John Pierson, a former search-and-recovery specialist and martial arts expert who had won a few belts in the early days of ultimate fighting.* Pierson began by teaching us how to run our guns. He presented his to us in profile and lectured on its features, holding it stationary in the air and pivoting around it like a mime or a pole dancer to keep from muzzling us. By lunch we knew the three secrets of good shooting—sight alignment, sight

 picture, trigger control—and we had practiced loading, unloading, chamber check/ mag check, and we knew the Weaver grip, because this was a Weaver school, though if we preferred the Isoscles or the Chapman we could do those too.

Students loaded magazines while Pierson talked, and that insect crackle of rounds clicking into place, that sound of grave

---

* Plato, it may be worth noting, was reportedly a two-time gold medalist in "pankration," the ultimate fighting of the early Olympic games, a tradition sometimes attributed to Lycurgus.

preparation, undermined the humor that Pierson attempted to use to spice up his lectures. His best jokes were always about homosexuality. Not lashing out at homosexuals, but citing homosexual tendencies in himself, which, because he was barrel-chested and battle ready, was so ridiculous that it was impossible to overlook the irony, to un-get the joke. Yet toward the end of our first day, Pierson wondered aloud whether he'd lost his touch with a gag, which prompted another stab at humor from one of my classmates.

"It's hard to laugh at a man carrying a gun."

This fell flat, too.

Probably tension had left us feeling unwitty. It was time to go hot range, fly some brass. We walked down to the closed end of our U of pinkish berms, where our audience of silhouette targets awaited their doom. We started out delivering controlled pairs to the chest from three meters, concentrating on the three secrets and focusing on the front sight of our guns. You could mess up trigger control in a couple ways: mashing or milking. Mashing meant you were yanking on the trigger, and your aim went high and right. Milking meant you were pulling too hard with your off hand, and you went low and left. I was a masher. I was a masher because the explosion of the gun, the sudden angry punch of it, scared the living piss out of me. The first time a gun went off beside me, I almost fell down. I shivered in the desert heat. The discharge of the Glock in my hand felt less like the ejaculation of the cock I wished I had than like a sudden violent spasm of life in some dead thing I was holding. In other words, it was still Freud, but it was neither sex nor death—it was the uncanny. It was difficult to learn to shoot well, because the way to learn to shoot well was to become comfortable with the uncanniness of it: Make a vise of your hands, align the sights, concentrate on the target only in the blurry distance beyond your eye's depth of field, ease back on the trigger, slow pull to a sudden break. Let the gun surprise you.

I needed help when we backed up to five meters and lifted our aim to the head box, the cranio-ocular cavity where the skull was softest. I kept getting hits that might have only stunned my bad guy. Mashing. An instructor stepped in beside me, placed a palm at my back, and told me to relax my finger and fixate on the front sight. He laid his own finger overtop my trigger finger. Concentrate, he said. His finger pressed into mine, his sweat-wet flesh spreading over my knuckle like warm putty. Relax. Keep the sights aligned. I was trembling. I felt the fingers of his other hand dig into the knobs of my vertebrae. Don't look at the target. Align the sights, wait for the break. Pressure. The gun went off. We did it again.

I gave my bad guy nostrils.

128

"I'll be happy to talk to you about Front Sight, and how I started Front Sight, but that's about as far back as I go."

In the late 1980s, a young chiropractor named Dr. Ignatius Piazza moved to northern California to open a practice. He had a plan going in. He went door-to-door to introduce himself to the community, person by person, and when he opened his business he already had more weekly appointments than his competition had lined up in years. He and his wife were soon able to purchase a home in an upscale neighborhood. One night not long after they moved in, they were having a quiet evening watching *Wheel of Fortune* when suddenly they heard gunshots, screeching tires, bullets hitting the house. Piazza and his wife fell to the ground. They had a gun safe upstairs, a whole arsenal under lock and key. But what good was it? Crouched and hiding in his own home, Piazza wondered what all the trips to the range had been for if he couldn't even get to his guns when he needed them. What if this had been a home invasion scenario and not just some random drive-by? By Piazza's own account,  becoming a victim of gun violence was the "revelation" that sent him on a "quest for training."

He hadn't come from gun roots. His family was antigun, and that was all he would say of them. He told me all this in Aptos, California, at the restaurant of a resort about a mile from his home. He had agreed to speak with me only after I completed my course at Front Sight and on the condition that we meet in a public place. I was determined not to like Piazza. I was determined not to like him because in Front Sight promotional material Piazza bragged of his ability to appeal to the antigun media, turn them to his cause. But I kind of did like him at first. His whole manner exuded what Front Sight literature called "the comfort of skill at arms." He was sort of okay to be around. We had been seated at a table in the sun, and I took off my light sport coat. The room was warm. Piazza left his leather jacket on and ordered a steaming bowl of clam chowder. He was a cool customer.

After the drive-by, he started traveling to gun schools. There were a few: Chuck Taylor's American Small Arms Academy; Colonel Jeff Cooper's American Pistol Institute; Massad Ayoob's Lethal Force Institute; Clint Smith's Thunder Ranch. In just his second course Piazza recognized the market's untapped potential: a large percentage of returning students and a rich demographic of doctors, lawyers, and business owners. An atmosphere built more on an IBM model, he suspected, would yield greater returns than the boot camp treatment you got from the jarhead types.

"Did that part of it ruffle your feathers?"

"Nah. Nothing ruffles my feathers. I mean, I was a chiropractor, for God's sake! I came into a community that had two hundred chiropractors and I met six thousand people to introduce myself. After an experience like that, nothing ruffles your feathers."

"Right, sure. Sure."

His training proceeded quickly. As he accumulated expert certificates, he began to search for the next level of validation. But it wasn't like you could get a doctorate in firearms training. There was only a public challenge. In 1981, Chuck Taylor had published the Four Weapon Combat Master test, a well-nigh impossible bar exam for would-be shootists. Twenty or thirty men had attempted it, but no one had passed. Piazza trained for six months. He rented out an entire school for himself. Handgun, shotgun, rifle, submachine gun. The intensity of the training was instruction itself in what a better shooting school should offer students. Piazza was thirty-three years old when witnesses verified that he had become, after Taylor, the world's second Four Weapon Combat Master.

He set about creating Front Sight much in the same way he'd set up his practice. Visited six hundred gun-shop owners in California, established a network to market the new school. The first Two-Day Defensive Handgun course was offered in Bakersfield in April 1996, and by December of the same year Front Sight had more students than the original school Piazza attended.

It took two years to find a site large enough to keep up with the expanding student body. The 550 acres outside Pahrump, Nevada, was as close as you could get to California without having to worry about obeying its laws.

"I didn't need the 550 acres for the training facility, but I did need room for expansion. And I thought, I've got this land, and I've got this growing student base. There are golf resort communities, there are equestrian communities, there are automobile racing communities, there are aviation communities. Let's have a gun community."

"What did people think?"

"Depends on who you were talking to. If they were a dyed-in-the-wool Second Amendment advocate, they thought it was a great idea. If they were antigun, they cringed—which was perfect. Because this was not for everybody. It was only for people who truly understand the importance of the Second Amendment, understand the importance of firearms ownership, and want what we provide. And they're coming to us in droves."

It had been twenty years since I fired a gun. My brother, Peter— the stoic homesteader of Utopia Road—had once earned extra money for his young family by trading guns in Arizona. This was years after the Wildlife Rescue Center. And it was years before Peter fought in a war and wound up in a career in counter-terrorism, years before our politics diverged. He took me shooting once when I passed through town. We hiked out onto an Indian reservation with semiautomatic rifles. I blew out my eardrum and have tinnitus to this day.

In Nevada, I stayed nights in a motel in a tiny town called Bonnie Springs that once upon a time was the last water stop for wagons headed into Death Valley. Now the whole town was dedicated to a primitive amusement park: mock gunfights, bank heists gone bad, erupted periodically on its Old West main street, and there were hangings at noon, 2:30, and 5:00 sharp. The town's petting zoo was a rest home for African cattle and South American hares retired from better petting zoos. To me there was nothing so utopian as a geriatric swan tipping its head ninety degrees to snip rabbit food from the palm of my hand.

128

I drove back to Front Sight for day two.

I arrived early for some extra dry fire practice. I worked on my aggressive lean. It was cool in the morning, but that afternoon accumulated heat pressure would shatter a window of someone's minivan. All of Front Sight was dirt, piled into artificial dunes like risen bread or flattened for roads as hot and hard as a griddle. Beneath the maze was a tunnel complex for urban scenarios, and in the middle of it was a $3 million, three-story obstacle course that was sometimes rented out for corporate team-building seminars. Pierson's class trickled in. Radiologists and tax attorneys and machinists and gynecologists. Some had come in groups. A young couple on a weekend escape. A man and his pastor. A group of old friends vacationing together. The men had names like Lou, Seth, Rod, Con, Vaughn, Cole, Corey, Rich, Alec, Rob, Morgan, Ryan, Craig, Bert, Reed, Walt, Doyle, Gordon, Jared. There were two types: chiseled figures attempting to live up to reputations cultivated so far only with words, and quiet nerds who were often better shots and more accurate with their after-action drills. T-shirts in the group broke an unspoken taboo on political small-talk: Annoy a Liberal; The Second Amendment—America's Original Homeland Security; Pain Is Weakness Leaving the Body; Sniper Golf—Where Every Shot Is a Hole in One; Truth Comes in the Form of a 6 to 9 Round Burst.

In the morning we worked on tactical reloads, which Pierson called an administrative function of running one's gun. This was typical. The language of Front Sight reveled in idiom, hyperbole, euphemism. If you screwed up your tac reload, Pierson said, you got yourself a bandage and a sad face on your medical report. The technical word for that was—bad. At that point, don't bother running, you'll just die tired. The other thing to worry about was what to expect when you got your hits on a bad guy on some go-fast drug. It took fourteen to twenty-eight seconds before blood loss to the brain affected performance, and that was the rationale behind the Mozambique (controlled pair to the chest, one to the head), because, Pierson said, there had never been a shot to the head box that "went unrewarded." No, wait, that sounded a little vicious. That didn't "have the desired effect." Either way, he said, you gotta finish off what you gotta finish off, and if you didn't your only chance would be if your bad guy died laughing.

The talk turned to concealed weapons. We'd already started working on presentation from concealment, drawing from cover, flipping back garments that we might wear in the states that offered conceal/carry permits. The class was curious about what kind of ammo Pierson preferred for his own CW. This led to some discussion of brands of ammo that tended to jam and a more philosophical comparison of the relative merits of .45 hardball and 9-mil hollow point. Pierson had some definite thoughts on this, having done some work of his own on wound channels in flesh. To be honest, he said, he didn't like the 14:9 ratio of gelatin to bone used in most ballistic studies. He intended to make his own body out of cow ribs and broomsticks to see what really happens.

"I need to find out for myself. I really do."

132

At lunch there were videos and lectures. The pitch to join the First Family was unrelenting. There was film of a grand First Family party at Front Sight from a few Fourths of July ago. Images of fireworks and awestruck children, waving flags and happy couples, a group sing-along of "God Bless America" set to a patriotic montage. Piazza did not have the comfort of skill at choir, though his wife did. The movie was followed by a lecture on the "color code of mental awareness," sort of a personal security rating system devised by Piazza. You should only be condition white when you were sleeping, the lecturer told us. Yellow wasn't paranoia, it was awareness. Go orange when you spot something that just doesn't seem right. Red, present and deliver a controlled pair. Black is muscle memory—get your hits, keep your gun running.

Mostly, life was condition yellow.

The student body took in the movies and lectures both with a stunned stoicism, a rustle of paper food wrappers, an audible group chew, and the burbling of whatever folks were using to hydrate. I had begun an informal survey to see what people thought of living in the town of Front Sight once it was complete. A number of students were enthusiastic. At lunch I sat across from a cryptological technician who had brought his wife and three daughters to Front Sight. He'd bought each of the girls a Springfield XDM (eXtreme Duty, Mega-capacity magazine) and now they were learning to use them. I nodded over at the model.

"Do you think you could live there?"

"Oh, you mean the cult?" He was kidding—the crucifix he wore in his left earlobe jiggled as he giggled.

In the afternoon, Pierson's class had its turn with Front Sight's Dalí-inspired installation piece: twenty freestanding doors in a grid out on the hard dirt. Pierson described the "fatal funnel" that resulted whenever a gunfight required you to pass through a narrow opening. There was only so much you could do about it. We practiced throwing open the doors, stepping and trailing, slicing the pie of our environments, and proceeding calmly and surely into the fatal funnel. After that we returned to the range to draw from concealment and take dedicated headshots. Pierson had us on a stopwatch now; we'd begun practicing for the tests of day four. By the end of day two, the backs of my legs were sunburned and there were nicks in my hands from running my reluctant gun, but I was beginning to feel some intimation of mastery, something not quite comfort, but at least I knew why I had a gun on my hip. I had moved from mashing to milking, but it was improvement. The goal of Front Sight was not to make a world without fear, I realized. The goal was equality of fearsomeness. I began to feel fearsome in the same way, I supposed, a change to better habits makes one feel wholesome. Late in the afternoon I partnered up with an older woman named Brenda whose husband was taking a shotgun class while she stuck with handgun training. Brenda's head shots were perfect. But she had a little difficulty drawing from concealment. She admired my own progress on this count. She pointed out that now, when Pierson turned the targets and we all went for our hips, mine was the first shot fired on the relay.

"You're *fast*," she said.

133

"In your class a few months ago there were three hundred students. In five days, we'll have five hundred and fifty—more than half of them brand-new. You know, you're not really our market. You need to understand that. You're here because the market intrigues you, but you're not it. You don't have a gun safe full of guns. You don't see the Second Amendment as the most important of all the amendments, that without the Second Amendment we don't have freedom of speech or anything else.

That's the mind-set of people like me. And those are the people who are going to embrace the community, the hotel, the time-share opportunities. It's just a matter of putting everything together and launching it all. I've had opportunities to sell Front Sight half a dozen times. For millions of dollars. But Front Sight's never been about the money. It's been about having a Mecca for the people that still have the blood of the Founding Fathers running through their veins. There's plenty of money to be made, but that's not the issue. The issue is completing the project without compromising anything."

"Do you think we're living in a kind of low-grade totalitarianism? That we've suffered dystopian slippage from the freedoms granted in the founding documents?"

"Without a doubt, we are moving toward a dependence on government, and once a majority of the population is dependent on the government there's no way to turn that around, because people will not vote against their dependency. Utopia is a situation of idealism, where everything is great. Well, I would say, for myself, and for my students: We don't need a lot. We just need to be free. Free to do what we choose to do that doesn't adversely affect anybody else. Everything else is secondary. If you can simply be free to pursue your life as you want to pursue it, you'll always be happy. Simple as that."

"I'd like to read you a quote from H. G. Wells."

"Okay."

" 'But in truth, a general prohibition in a state may increase the sum of liberty, and a general permission may diminish it. . . . Suppose there existed even the limited freedom to kill in vendetta, and think what would happen in our suburbs. Consider the inconvenience of two households in a modern suburb estranged and provided with modern weapons of precision, the inconvenience not only to each other, but to the neutral pedestrian, the practical loss of freedoms about them.' "

"Can you read that again?"

As I read the quote a second time, Piazza sat up and shrugged his shoulders, adjusting the heavy sleeves of his leather coat. Until that moment I had not thought of the coat as a concealment garment, and now I regretted my own limp sport coat hanging across the arm of my chair. Piazza tended to play fast and loose with facts—he distrusted polling data on firearms ownership in America—and he brushed Wells aside with the evidence of Florida, whose conceal/carry law, he claimed, had reduced crime statewide. As well, Wells didn't account for the kind of person drawn to Front Sight.

"You're dealing with the cream of the crop. It's not the Hatfields and the McCoys. These issues don't occur, and that's why Front Sight will be the safest town in America. I think it was Heinlein who said, 'An armed society is a polite society.' Have you heard this quote?"

"Yes."

"Yeah, well, what does it mean? Say you and I are sitting here. You're a Democrat and I'm a Republican. Now say we get into a heated debate. All right. If you know I'm armed, and I know you're armed, then we're going to be a little cautious with our freedom of speech, aren't we?"

"Yeah."

"We're not going to insult each other's wives, we're not going to insult each other's mothers, we're not going to talk with street language. We're not going to do that, because there's always the potential that we could step over that line, that violence could occur, and you have the ability, and I have the ability, to hurt each other significantly. It's like the arms race. It's like the deterrence of two superpowers with nuclear weapons. Nobody wants to be the one who fires first, because it's destruction for both."

"Isn't that enforced morality? Isn't it choosing to be good from expedience?"

"Well, you and I are both good to each other here, right? We're good to each other because we're civilized, we're responsible, and because we've realized that you get more with a smile and good communication that you get with being a jerk. So it's a learned behavior. Firearms in the hands of law-abiding citizens enforce that learned behavior. You don't want to mess with somebody who has the ability to take your life in a moment. And they know you have that same ability. So it does force good manners. If a bank robber walks into a bank and the tellers are armed, and the customers are armed, how many times is that bank robber going to try that again? You see? It changes the whole perspective on crime and violence in the country. The best thing that could happen is, everybody's armed."

134

On day three I partnered up with a beefy man named Rick. I'd heard he'd been Special Forces, and I was curious about what one did on retiring from Special Forces.

"Extradition work."

"To the U.S.?"

"No."

"So that's—Border Patrol?"

Rick smiled. "No. Different company."

Day three range activities included controlled pairs and dedicated head shots for most of the morning. The staff delivered another hard sell for the First Family at lunch, and a fair percentage of the students appeared ready to buy in or upgrade existing memberships. We practiced malfunctions in the afternoon, the three things that can foul a weapon, and we were told to reserve fifty rounds of ammunition for the evening's night shoot. As the sun fell, we learned flashlight techniques—Rogers, Harrie, cigar-style—then fired controlled pairs at turning targets to the light of a full moon. Rick was disappointed when the shooting was done.

"Wasn't no fifty rounds."

"You were shooting them off pretty good there," I said.

Rick had fired far more bullets at each target than he was supposed to; none of the instructors stopped him. He took two steps and thought about it.

"Wasn't no fifty rounds."

Pierson walked us through some home invasion scenarios in the lecture that followed. Whatever's in your living room is insured, he reminded us. The irreplaceable stuff, your wife, your kids, that's all upstairs. And you can protect that stuff, he said, by, say, strategically positioning a light on your landing. The stairway would become your fatal funnel.

"It's like a tunnel," Pierson said. "Like the Spartans. They'd have to be crazy to come up those stairs."

He meant Leonidas and Thermopylae—not Lycurgus—but the class understood all the same.

135

"So utopia to me, and I believe to the people that support and attend Front Sight, is the ability to be free and pursue the happiness and the liberty that we choose to pursue. A comparison to Sparta? I particularly like the whole story of Sparta."

"You do?"

"Oh, absolutely. Absolutely. I think they were a bit harsh in their treatment of children that weren't perfect, but there's something to be said for that, as well, in that we coddle, here, in this country, people who are not able to perform to the levels of everybody else. It weakens us as a whole. But we're a compassionate people."

"The Spartans weren't particularly compassionate, were they?"

"No, absolutely not. But you know who people ran to when they needed somebody? Go tell the Spartan. So I like the story of Sparta. I really do. I realize that was a different time, and that we'll never see those days again unless some type of situation occurs that levels the playing field, and you have some of those communities created. But this country is soft. As a whole, it's soft. It's soft because we've become complacent over time. You talk to people in their eighties, and you find those who saw life in its full spectrum. You talk to someone who is seventeen or twenty-five—their concerns are much different from those who fought for our freedom. We benefit from the blood they spilled, yet we have no idea of the hardship they went through. And you look at our country now, and you wonder, could it sustain something like that? Yeah, it could. But there would be a lot of soft, weak people that wouldn't make it. They just wouldn't. We'll have to wait around and see. See how all this shakes out. But one thing's for sure, Front Sight students are going to do fine, because they have the ability, and the tools, to defend themselves, no matter what happens. And that's really what we provide, that comfort of skill at arms. It all comes back to that."

136

Pierson's class had fully bonded by the morning of day four. Students exchanged contact information to stay in touch and snapped portraits of one another, smiling, arms draped around the freestanding demonstration silhouette Pierson used for his lectures.

We started the final day with a shooting competition, a tournament that by the luck of the draw pitted brother against brother, husband against wife. Draw from cover, one to the head box of a hostage taker at three meters, singles to the chest of two accomplices farther back. My first opponent, Mike, tapped my elbow in congratulations when I made all three hits. I lost in the second round to a man who used tai chi to prepare for my challenge. It scared me; I shot the hostage.

I sat with a man named Jayson for the rest of the tournament. I'd partnered with Jayson for part of day two. He was a kindly, portly man. He was the one who had brought his pastor to Front Sight, and he was a firearms instructor himself, offering classes required by Minnesota's conceal/carry legislation. As the tournament proceeded, I noted something odd. Many students were hitting the hostage taker but missing the accomplices, which were easier shots.

"Yeah. I think they're looking at the target," Jayson said.

Which hit me like Piazza's drive-by revelation. The meta-phor in the subtext of the pedagogy: to concentrate on the front sight, to shoot well, was to ignore down-range, or long-range, consequences of your actions. In other words, don't plan. Don't think ahead. Absolve yourself of intent. To consider your target, even to look at it, was to risk missing it.

Out in the blank desert, we all stumbled on another revelation—Zoroaster's. We were the good guys, they were the bad guys. It didn't matter who they were or what they'd done, you'd already made that decision before you went from condition orange to condition red, before you presented and executed your drills. Front Sight was not a utopia of intentionality; it was res-ignation to dystopia. Which is to say it was not earnestly utopian at all. Front Sight was preposterous. Piazza was preposterous. One needed to go no further than Bonnie Springs to note that the last time everyone was armed in America had not resulted in a marked decrease in bank robberies. Piazza's solution to a world edging toward totalitarianism was to create one of his own, to reinvent the benevolent despot who would transform the psychology of his populace. His utopia was dystopia by de-sign rather than accident. He didn't get the joke, and he didn't mean it earnestly, either.

Front Sight looked back to a Second Amendment golden age, and forward to a postapocalypse in which the best world was the one that lasted longest, surrounded by enemies. That's a witless read of *Utopia*, but it's not utopian. It's not what became of utopia after More's joke was un-got by "fools" more earnest than he was. Utopia *is* for everyone; it must be. Utopia *is* condi-tion white. If civilization is to mean anything at all, it must mean the ability to live without fear of your fellow citizens, not because you know how to confront fear, not because you know how to combat it, but because community has been achieved among not just the like-minded, but collectively. This is what Aristotle meant, reacting to Plato, in his insistence that the "happy city in isolation . . . would not be constituted with any view to war or the conquest of enemies—all that sort of thing must be excluded." That this exclusion is difficult to achieve has been met with a variety of poisonous ideologies, all of which boil down to the curious suggestion that the unintentional is a *better* form of intent. But sham propositions that promise magical stability—good versus evil, mutual assured destruction, free markets—are simply another way of focusing on the front sight, another way of thinking of yourself before others. You cannot dress the whore of greed in the pinafore of competition and call her virtuous. You cannot pay yourself dividends and cite the greater good. Such philosophies are utopian only in that they are self-congratulatory—they call resignation pragmatism, hopelessness honor: hold steady, shoot the bad guys, but don't look at them, because if you do you might miss. And don't expect thanks because you've opted for faith.

Prowess with a gun, like prowess with statecraft, is Job's dilemma. Your sacrifice will go unrewarded.

137

Before we began our final tests, Pierson handed out teacher evaluation forms and explained that we did not have to give him perfect scores across the board. Then he drew down on us with an imaginary gun made from his fist and a crimped trigger finger. He panned across us, the only time he muzzled us with anything.

The class laughed.

I wound up next to Rick on the relay for our tests. Controlled pairs and dedicated head shots on turning targets from a variety of distances. I was ready and confident. But I was also sad. I was sad that the dystopian spirit had welled up in me as well as or better than the counterpart I wanted to nurture. In the end, I was still a child of Utopia Road. My sadness did not affect my performance. I was a better shot than the bounty hunter beside me. In the ceremony that followed, Rick was annoyed that my graduation certificate lacked the silver sticker my score should have earned.

"You should complain," he said.

The gathered throng of students gave the instructional staff a standing ovation.

"Until next time we meet," the operations manager said, "stay in condition yellow."

The desert had depleted me. At the airport I got half drunk on half a beer. As I walked out of a restroom, I swung my satchel over my hip, hiking it past the imaginary Glock I could still feel like a phantom limb. My psychology had changed. I was reluctantly potent. I struggled against my awareness. I was quick on the draw. I looked at my fellow travelers, innocents all, hoping foolishly for a safe and comfortable world.

I will take the dedicated head shot. I will concentrate on the front sight, slow pull to a sudden break. I will present from concealment. I will deliver to the soft part of the skull.

A HOME

The utopian mentality, I should repeat, is withering away. Its intellectual status sank to the level of a pathetic adolescent gibberish surviving in leftist sects. . . . It is legitimate to ask whether this demise of utopia, however justifiable in terms of the gruesome history of utopian politics, may be seen as a net gain.

—LESZEK KOLAKOWSKI,

"The Death of Utopia Reconsidered"

The worldly, the domestic, the wild: is this not the very tripartition of social desire? It is anything but surprising that I turn from this Bayonnaise garden to the fictive, utopian spaces of Jules Verne and Fourier. (The house is gone now, swept away by the housing projects of Bayonne.)

—ROLAND BARTHES

Before we worked at the Wildlife Rescue Center, my brother and I used to fish at a master-planned park in Utopia Road. The park had a name, but we called it Fake Lake.

Six months after my meeting with Piazza, I returned to Utopia Road. My sister, Amy, lived nearby. On our way back to our old neighborhood, we stopped at Fake Lake. Willows gripped the shore of a pond that was equipped with a filtration system. There were turtles out in force, ducks fooled by the waterfall, and while we strolled a great, gangly heron came soaring in and plopped down like an angel on the waterline. I used to bring girls here. You could hear traffic on I15 up the hill, but it was not an unpleasant spot. It was the pleasantness that made it unnatural.

My sister had brought her camera, but she wasn't sure how to work the technology. We squabbled over it. Peter was not with us because he had been called into another war. He was in Baghdad, in the Green Zone, and I found it hard to imagine a better phrase to describe what had been done to the utopian spirit.

Our old neighborhood was in poor shape. The road needed new tar, mustard plants had laid siege to the landscaping, and street signs were in disrepair.

The couple who had bought our house on Utopia Road thirty-two years before still lived there. Their terrier, an efficient guard, was newer than that. The barking made it difficult to communicate the purpose of our visit when the lady of the house answered the door. Her husband suffered from obsessive-compulsive disorder, she said, so we couldn't come inside. She would meet us in the backyard.

They had once been burgled, she told us. The robbers had been caught red-handed and tried to make their escape through a window just above the spot where the old photo of my brother and me had been taken. Amy snapped new pictures. The woman told us stories. They'd had problems with rats—the neighbors' olive trees attracted them. She said we could stay as long as we liked. She had been dressing for church when we rang the bell. We lingered a short while.

In 1954, forty years and two wars after H. G. Wells eulogized the grammatical death of utopia, C. S. Lewis approached the matter anew. *Utopia* was not a political book at all, he claimed. It was fiction, satire. Its riddle, he said, became "intelligible and delightful as soon as we take it for what it is—a holiday work . . . which starts many hares and kills none."

In other words, Utopia was of the same genus as Middle Earth, Never-Never Land, and Narnia. Escapism. Don't take the joke too seriously.

But was that what More meant in the end? Was *Utopia* a fantasy for children? Lewis had described his era better than he described the book, an era in which More was now a saint (he was canonized in 1935), an era desperate to forgive itself for having turned *Utopia* into a prank with horrific results. Maybe that was the gag of it. Utopia is the sardonic joke the world played on itself. We were all Mores, fools, and those who had earnestly imagined a better world built from good intentions were simply foolish. This is consistent with the disclaimer of "More" at the end of *Utopia*, and some commentators have suggested that's the whole point: Not even *Utopia* was a utopia. Indeed, it was the first dystopian novel.

But maybe *that's* the joke.

Yet why shouldn't the history of violent utopias and the tendency of visions to coronate their visionary invalidate utopia as rhetorical red herring—perhaps the reddest herring of all?

Utopia itself is a human force, a Vril (read: will), an engine, a mechanism that drives whatever progress human beings are capable of making. Like any power it has the potential to run amok. But we do not stop using knives because we occasionally stab each other or cut ourselves; we do not unplug our lamps because children are sometimes electrocuted; and we should not douse the utopian flame because fires sometimes destroy pretty landscapes or burn phalansteries to the ground. The choice is not between utopia and some fool's proposition that not trying is a better form of trying. The latter, anyway, is not an alternative to utopian thought but only the ugliest version of it, a version in which societies on the decline indulge as the ground rots beneath their feet. The truth of utopia is that you cannot choose to be utopian or not, for no one makes a plan, or establishes an ideology, or imagines a future that is not an attempt to improve on the plan, or the politics, or the past it replaces. The joke of *Utopia*, it turns out, is not that it is folly to try to make a better world. More had offered neither an indictment nor a blueprint—though *Utopia* was taken for both. His dichotomy of fools called for a punch line, a synthesis, in reply: The failure of good intentions should not be met with inaction, but with further good intentions, with *better* intentions. The wit and fantasy of More, of all utopian thought, wounded you in the sense that it penetrated you, got in there with the gelatin and the broomsticks, and made you vulnerable to the idea that where you are, wherever you are, isn't good enough, that progress, intentional progress, is possible, and that the imperfect can be made more perfect, and the perfect more perfect still.

The butt of the joke of *Utopia* was always us.

140

Earnest utopians are late saints: sad, sweet martyrs.

Image Credits

Pp. 7 and 13, copyright The Frick Collection, New York; p. 34, courtesy of Dave Foreman; p. 44, from Paul Martin's *Pleistocene Extinctions: The Search for a Cause,* by Paul Martin, copyright Yale University Press; pp. 62, 63, and 66, Catherine Michele Adams; p. 110, courtesy of Jean-Philippe Zopinni; p. 116, copyright Artists Rights Society, New York/ADAGP, Paris/FLC; p. 117, John Berkey for *Popular Mechanics* (popularmechanics.com); p. 121, courtesy of the Lyndon Baines Johnson Presidential Library; p. 122, courtesy of America World City Corporation; p. 123, Catherine Michele Adams; p. 127, courtesy of Knut Kloster, Jr.; p. 139, Art Resource, New York; p. 150, courtesy of *Cabinet Magazine*; p. 179, courtesy of Cittaslow International; p. 200, two images, Catherine Michele Adams; p. 201, courtesy of *Cabinet Magazine*; p. 208, copyright Frank Lloyd Wright Foundation, Scottsdale, Arizona, and Artists Rights Society, New York/ADAGP, Paris/FLC, and Art Resource, New York; p. 209, Artists Rights Society, New York; p. 215, Catherine Michele Adams; pp. 243, 244, and 247, courtesy of Dr. Ignatius Piazza.